Film Acting

ARCO FILM SERIES

The Techniques and History of Acting for the Camera

The basis of any technique must be "truth."
—Maggie Smith

Film Acting

ARCO FILM SERIES

The Techniques and History of Acting for the Camera

MARY ELLEN O'BRIEN

ARCO PUBLISHING, INC.
New York

Published by Arco Publishing, Inc.
215 Park Avenue South, New York, N.Y. 10003

Library of Congress Cataloging in Publication Data

O'Brien, Mary Ellen.
    Film acting.

    Includes index.
    1. Moving-picture acting. I. Title.
PN1995.02   791.43′028   82–4013
ISBN   0–668–05240–6 (Cloth   Edition)   AACR2
ISBN 0–668–05251–1 (Paper Edition)

Printed in the United States of America

10   9   8   7   6   5   4   3   2   1

All photographs were supplied courtesy of *The Film Journal* (Hollins
College, VA 24020) and the British Film Institute (London).

for
John L. O'Brien

CONTENTS

INTRODUCTION

What is good film acting?

At the end of *The Godfather*, Marlon Brando as Don Corleone plays with his small grandson in the garden. He takes a bit of orange and sticks it into his mouth to resemble false teeth, then grimaces and chases the boy through the tomato patches. Giggling, the boy sprays this powerful figure, a godlike father, with an insecticide . . . and then the game continues, ending with the death of the Don, a pathetic monster made human by a heart attack.

This is an inspired moment of film acting. Why? The director and the actor in this particular scene chose a physical prop and a setting that are startling, yet appropriate; both are comic and sinister in delineating the image of the godfather who is also a harvester of men's lives—one who decides who lives and dies within his realm of organized crime. The child's game of "hide and seek," and the use of a mask (simply created with the orange peel), reveal the comforting and threatening traits in Don Corleone. Thus, the spectator sees two sides of a character, which is aesthetically reassuring as well as stimulating.

We go to the movies to be entertained and to enjoy the artistic work of the filmmaker and his collaborators: actors, designers, technicians, and musicians. There in the dark we are much more likely to accept various kinds of images and identities along with the popcorn, soda, and candy than we are in a more formal environment, such as the legitimate theatre. We are encouraged by the dreamlike quality of film images to absorb meaning and metaphor as readily as we learned to ride bicycles in childhood—through the repetition of sensory experience.

For many Americans who were children in the thirties, forties, and fifties, "going to the movies" was an integral part of the week, just as watching the *Sesame Street–Mister Rogers–Electric Company* TV complex is for youngsters today. In my own St. Louis neighborhood kids went to the movies four times a week: on Wednesday for "Merchants' Gift Night" (when a raffle for groceries and toys was held following the movie); on Friday for "Westerns"; on Saturday we screamed during the murder mysteries and groaned during the love stories (using those moments to get closer to our boyfriends under the pretense of fear or boredom); and on Sunday we released ourselves from the sin of the week by laughing and hooting during the adventure and cartoon matinees.

In that visually sensual world, as freely and totally as in dreams, we shared our identities with the Cisco Kid and Charlie Chan. It didn't matter to us who played the parts or how well they acted, since each of us was the other half of any characterization and could do no wrong. I can still become the character in a World War Two film who had his face changed by plastic surgery into Oriental features in order to become a spy and serve the United States, but who as a result also lost his Japanese friend.

This childhood feeling of having been part of every character seen in the movies can lead to a willingness to accept a broader range of acting styles and characters, to digest characterization as food for the imagination as you sit alone in the dark. In the world of stage and literature this is called empathy. To many in the film world it's called "making a dollar." The business term is regrettable because it tends to negate the aesthetic power of film and film actors, which is twice as potent as that of the stage. Film itself—in its motion of montage, angles, and cuts—has the capability of affecting us with the elements of dreams.

Having gone to the movie shows to watch strong stories unfold, to see heroes battle their enemies and heroines rescue their families, to cheer Lassie and Cheetah (for me as vivid as any human star), you come to accept as viable works of art many different kinds of movies, to expect different reactions to each one, and to "pass" on the ones that are made for the dollar. Someone out there will like them.

As children in the forties, for instance, our demands were fulfilled by Shirley Temple, and Abbott and Costello. In the seventies, after unacceptable wars and shocking assassinations, our demands as moviegoers became more complex and less naive. Yet we are still fascinated by the intricate plot, by the star actor in any story, by political films (perhaps more subtly constructed now), and by intimate biographies.

Personality is communicated so strongly on film that it is unwise to make any final statements regarding film acting, an elusive art that incorporates not only a wide spectrum of styles, but also the potency of an almost unlimited variety of different faces of actors, all of whom affect us sensually.

Just as each of us sits alone in a movie theatre, responding individually to the motion and physical characteristics of actors (human or animal) as well as to color and locale, so this book is an individual response, an attempt to investigate the nature of screen performance.

I
Panorama

1

CONTEMPORARY FILM ACTING

Film today offers infinite possibilities for young actors. No longer are audiences required to pledge allegiance only to actors who represent some ideal form of beauty packaged for them by producers and directors. Today the range of film stars includes all types: the beautiful, the bad, the sweet, and the ugly. Actors and actresses such as Dustin Hoffman, Charles Bronson, Faye Dunaway, Barbra Streisand, Richard Dreyfuss, Jessica Lange, Maggie Smith, Roy Scheider, Marsha Mason, Michael Murphy, Jon Voight, Sigourney Weaver, Sissy Spacek, Jane Fonda, Vanessa Redgrave, Robert Redford, Jack Nicholson, Gene Hackman, Walter Matthau, Glenda Jackson, Al Pacino, Robert De Niro, Madeline Kahn, and Burt Reynolds represent the new types in film of the eighties.

Tall women are cast with shorter men, as in the case of Vanessa Redgrave and Dustin Hoffman in *Agatha*, and nobody has to stand in a hole or on a box for love scenes. Young film actors today can be suave, shy, crude, intellectual, or vivacious. They can have big ears, little ears, or ears that stick out. They can have big noses, little noses, crooked or straight noses. They can wear makeup or not. They can be fat, thin, or in-between.

The endless variety of personality and physical type on screen in leading roles opens up more opportunities for actors who are not examples of the classical ideal of beauty. Films today are more complex partially because the actors themselves are more interesting in appearance and subtler in performance.

Actors such as De Niro, Pacino, and Hoffman are often

Jessica Lange as Angelique and Roy Scheider as director Joe Gideon in All That Jazz.

classified as the "anti-hero" type. These men are not handsome in the traditional Hollywood sense of glamour. They are beautiful in that they rivet our attention to them. They are actors whose thoughts spring from layers of emotion, and so communicate a thoughtfulness, a seriousness about what is happening to them as characters in the story.

Actresses such as Sally Field, Goldie Hawn, Marsha Mason, Susan Anspach, Blythe Danner, Jill Clayburgh, Jane Fonda, Sigourney Weaver, and Margot Kidder all have recently played women who are capable, intelligent, and feminine, but whose sense of identity doesn't rest or end with their mirror images, women whose edges are a little rough and ragged.

The variety of actors in film today seems to spring from a focus away from physical beauty to a focus on the psychophysical. Audiences are more interested in what lies beneath the surface than in the surface itself. Films like *Norma Rae, The Great Santini, Coal-Miner's Daughter,* and *Agatha* draw intricate portraits of complex men and women. An actor's face today must reveal more than exquisite features enhanced by excellent makeup; the face must reflect the inner decisions and complex conflicts of modern characters.

There may be many causes for this recent attention on the psychophysical. Some of the attention may be the result of the social and political revolution of the sixties, which turned our attention from the appearance of things to the substance of things. Events around the globe in the past twenty years have shaken our traditional individual viewpoints and our collective identification as members of political, social, or geographical groups. We stumbled over the clay feet of politicians encased in government scandals. Our eyes burned with the televised sight of war and assassination attempts. We faced the unhappy facts of the conditions endured by newly observed minorities: women, the aging, Chicanos, and others. We looked inward through encounter systems and founded the "Me Generation." We tracked youthfulness with a vengeance, and have made children into miniature versions of the encountered, analyzed, Rolfed, "me."

Movies reflect society's interests and concerns and either progress to deal with the more important recent revolutions or regress to exploit our fears and fantasies. The psychophysical

Sally Field in Norma Rae.

interest echoes in our acquaintance with encounter groups, Zen, charismatic religions, the "how-to" books of personal development, transcendental meditation, the martial arts, running, health foods, hot tubs, and biofeedback techniques.

As in any historical development, the pendulum of artistic activity swings in a wide arc. On one hand, the revolutionary changes in our living patterns allowed the production of films like *Julia, The Turning Point,* and *An Unmarried Woman;* on the other hand, our fears are exploited in films like the rash of cut-and-chop, slit-and-slash films. Films in the past twenty years have followed new directions in language, action, and theme.

Films in the tradition of *The Turning Point* and *Julia* have looked closely at the psychology of the female mind, and found it to be as intricate as that of the male mind. These films illuminate the courage of the woman, the complexity of the woman, and the humor of the woman. *Kramer vs. Kramer* and *Ordinary People* put families on the dissecting table and reveal that sex roles don't make the man or the woman.

Language in film is freer now than at any other point in history. Women, men, teenagers, and children explode expletives so often, we'll soon need to develop new ones out of boredom with the old. In fact, a rather trite signature of a "modern" film is the use of language once confined to more private locations.

Nudity in films is standard. In making up for the many years in which only females were seen in any stage of nudity, men are now appearing nude in vast numbers. A list of the male derrieres seen in the past ten years would be more impressive than needs recounting here. The old argument of whether the nudity "serves the story" is dated; we take for granted that it enhances the narrative, and enjoy it. Only one film has gone beyond mere nudity to capture the astounding kinetic attributes of the flesh beneath: Nicolas Roeg's *Don't Look Now.* This movie contains the most sensual and soulful pictorialization of love on film in a scene between the characters played by Julie Christie and Donald Sutherland.

Themes are more provocative in film, paralleling the break-throughs in the use of language and nudity. Witness *Apocalypse Now, Ordinary People, Norma Rae,* and *All That Jazz.* In these films we see and consider the following: the warmonger in a recreation of the Vietnam War; a mother so chilled by repression she cannot

communicate any love to her child; a good-time girl metamorphos-
ing into a labor leader risking her job and life; and a New York
choreographer drugging and working himself to an early death.
Films such as *The Great Santini* and *Blood Brothers* unrelentingly
unfold the truth of destructive family dynamics. The reality
exuded by these films in script and performances is a mixture of the
known and the unknowable. The acting—by Blythe Danner and
Robert Duvall in *The Great Santini,* and Tony Lo Bianco and
Richard Gere in *Blood Brothers*—is superb in the blend of natural-
ism and heightened realism. In neither film will be found improvisational acting for its own sake or for the sake of "style."

   The film industry took another route away from the sixties: it
gave us violence in a slick form, brutality in high-gloss wrapping—
the disaster film. We have seen bombs explode on hijacked planes,
and witnessed earthquakes and floods, the fiery destruction of
high-rises, and the sinking of ships. We have shared panic with
people attacked by killer bees and those who try to escape from
being placed in a coma and frozen for an organ bank. We have
struggled with aliens who invade human body systems to grow and
burst forth, we have fought 1940-style battles with invaders in
space ships, and we have had close encounters with friendly
visitors from outer space, visitors whose sense of inner peace
beckons to our ravaged psyches.

   These escapist films are balanced by those films reflecting a
consuming interest in life crises, the ensuing possibility of breakdown, and the struggle to overcome these personal adversities. The
passionate search for identity is the subject of several films of the
past ten years. Jill Clayburgh moves from dependence to indepen-
dence as the character in *An Unmarried Woman.* In the same film,
Michael Murphy limns a complicated portrait of a man seeking love
through manipulation of others. In *Kramer vs. Kramer,* Dustin
Hoffman is forced by circumstances to make the happy discovery
of effective parenting. In these films and in *Starting Over* with Burt
Reynolds, divorce is a catalyst for personality crises, and change.

   Woody Allen's *Interiors* focused on the intimacy of death and
its effects on the women in a family. Stunted personalities of three
"losers" are documented in Robert Altman's *Three Women* with
Sissy Spacek, Shelley Duvall, and Janice Rule. Bergman's *Scenes
from a Marriage* unleashes the violence beneath the surface of a
faltering marital relationship.

Diane Keaton (l.), in her most subtle characterization, in Woody Allen's Interiors.

In these sorts of films, the actor must be capable of revealing a duality of personality to develop the subtle themes and actions. There appear to be many contradictions in the personalities of the characters in these films. An actor must know how to communicate the imperfections of character subtly and clearly.

Modern film characters are constructions of contradiction, of duality, of nuance and subtlety. Modern film actors must themselves be sensitive to these contradictions, and must be adept at communicating them. At the same time they must be, or rather, appear to be, directly active in the moment. Beneath the straightforward surface must lie an introspective remoteness. Availability must coexist with elusiveness, violence with vulnerability. One aspect bleeds through the other, one aspect fades, revealing what lies beneath. This is the pentimento of characterization.

2

ORIGINS AND
HERITAGE: THE
SILENT FILM

In the earliest motion pictures there were few trained actors. The pioneer French filmmaker Louis Lumière often used members of his family, friends, or passers-by to "appear" in the action. His interest was not to create character or situation. He was intrigued by the mechanical capacity of the newly-invented *cinematographe* to capture movement on celluloid. The "player," as the actor was termed in these early films, was as important as a train engine or racing dog. An 1896 film screening at a New York City music hall, for instance, gave equal emphasis to footage of surf breaking and an umbrella dance performed by two young women.

Under the influence of innovators such as Georges Méliès and Edwin S. Porter, filming and editing methods developed to allow a plot, and more stage actors were encouraged to participate in this new art form. The stilted performance mannerisms, carried over from the theatre, appear artificial to us today because we are accustomed to a naturalistic acting style. Film techniques of the 1890s and early 1900s encouraged a less realistic brand of acting.

In his *The Rise of the American Film*, Lewis Jacobs lists some of the early filmmaking techniques which must have intruded upon the actor's concentration:

• The players had to face the camera and move horizontally, except when the movement was rapid. Then action was in diagonal relation to the camera in order to give the players more area.

11

This scene from D. W. Griffith's Way Down East illustrates the horizontal frieze effect of early cinema acting.

- Background action had to be slow and greatly exaggerated so it would register.
- Pantomime had to be exaggerated and over-deliberate; e.g. stares were held; starts were violent; speeches were mouthed with pronounced slowness.

In order for any actor to begin thinking about the creation of truthful characterization, he would have had to absorb these conventions so thoroughly that he no longer had to think about them and could focus his attention completely on the role. This is no easy task. Even today, film actors facing their first close-up find it difficult to absorb the conventions of the technical environment in which they must work.

Observing the acting in these early films we see the influence of the Delsarte method of acting—boldly signaled emotional and mental attitudes. François Delsarte tried to formulate a mechanics of speech and gesture during his career in the 1800s as a voice professor in Paris. He had himself lost his voice as a result of faulty instruction at the Paris Conservatoire in 1825, and he devoted his life to training actors in the coordination of speech to gesture. One of his pupils was the French actress, Rachel, who is still renowned for the naturalistic stage business she used as Lady MacBeth, such as licking imagined blood from her fingers in the sleepwalking scene.

In his *Random Notes* Delsarte remarked, for example, that "the mouth plays a part in everything evil which we would express, by a grimace which consists of protruding the lips and lowering the corners. If the grimace translates a concentric sentiment, it should be made by compressing the lips. . . . Any interrogation made with crossed arms must partake of the character of a threat." Rachel was able to translate his mechanical instructions into realistic playing which did indeed move the audience to "fear and trembling." By the end of the 19th century, the Delsarte method had attracted a number of American performers, who used his techniques to show the outer form and thereby reveal the inner form of emotion.

Many actors unfortunately exaggerated these physical techniques rather than converging their emotional experiences to a minute study of the role. The performances of a number of actors in films were obvious and over-physical. Tragic emotions were often played in a pathetic demeanor. Standardized makeup and gestures became signs and symbols substituting style for acting. Actors and actresses imitated each other and themselves.

In an early book on motion picture acting, author Jean Bernique advised the film actor to depend upon the "gleaming eye, the distended nostrils, the furrowed brow, or the compressed lips" to emphasize emotion. This emphasis on the external manifestation of emotion was common in the early 1900s. Beginning actors were trained to practice expressions which were pictured for them in books and magazines. Stars such as Mary Pickford, Earle Williams, and Lillian Gish posed for the still cameras, exhibiting expressions meant to embody bullying, cringing, denunciatory, artful, appalled, or vigilant attitudes.

Under the astute direction of D.W. Griffith, the first great American film artist, actresses such as Lillian and Dorothy Gish reordered the standardized methods into authentic and genuine experiences on film. Use of the eyes, for instance, had always been an important element in melodramatic playing on stage and screen. The Gish sisters let their eyes reveal on film the more important elements of feeling and sensuality. Their performances are moving in their simplicity of expression.

Other actors watching and analyzing their screen performances became aware of the dangers in emotional indulgence. British actor Cyril Maude vowed never to cast his eyes heavenward in a sanctimonious manner, concluding such a gesture was ugly on screen because it showed the whites of the eyes too plainly. Maude also believed it was essential to see oneself in makeup before shooting the film.

For actor George Pearson, the most difficult quality to attain on screen was also the backbone of successful film acting—repose.

As actors became more familiar with the results of acting on camera, they began to realize that "posing" was the worst thing an actor could do. Set expressions for set attitudes and situations were self-limiting. Actors were exhorted to be the character, to think, but not act out their emotions. It became evident that the eye of the camera could be a most terrible critic, revealing every weakness of those who acted before it. The camera would present objectively and ruthlessly the best and the worst of what an actor had to offer.

The physically overstated style of representing emotion by certain facial movements was criticized in a 1924 *Photoplay* photo-essay entitled "Running the Silent Scale—in which Dorothy Phillips tries her skill at the much maligned method of depicting dramatic moods for the camera. . . ." The reactions depicted by Phillips are generalized attitudes: fear, despair, faith, incredulity, repugnance, and coquetry. Such reactions were often required during screen tests of young actresses. The capitalization of the words in the article indicates the expected embellishment of response and stylized presentation of emotions which was the banner of early film acting. Today, it is anathema to "play a noun," and Paul Newman, among other modern actors trained in a variety of methods, including the Stanislavsky Method, advises young students to think in terms of active verbs: to convince, to inform, to humor.

Although we may still find much of the acting in D.W. Griffith's films too formal for our modern tastes, we are obliged to him for making extraordinary contributions to the development of film acting. Griffith used much greater care in casting films, searching for the right *type* to project what he wanted in the scenes. One of the rare directors who rehearsed scenes before shooting, he also decided to move the camera in for close-ups of the actors' faces. All of these innovations advanced the art of acting towards more naturalistic forms. Exaggerated expressions and movements appeared incongruous as well as false in close-ups. Griffith opened the door to the need for seeing thought illuminate the face. A critic of the time mentioned of Griffith's actors that they are "not small parties of puppets moving about the stage. . . . They are active photographs of thinking men and women. . . . You see what is passing in the minds of the actors and actresses."

Today we call this physical expression of thought "body language," which now tends to be more subtle in meaning and somewhat more a repression of anxiety than the body language of the 1916 to 1930 era. The visualization of body language in any era is one of the major potencies of film, leading the spectator to identify actors by some distinguishing physical trait, or by the screen character's name.

These giant screen images, powerfully evoking associations in the virgin audience of the twentieth century, began to take on living energy—and the star system was born. Actors and studios followed the inclination and capitalized on this youthful awareness in the audience. Ben Turpin, a slightly cross-eyed actor, said to one of his directors, "Shoot the eyes! Shoot the eyes! What do millions of people go to the movies for?" Roles were written or rewritten as types: "the sweet young thing whose mother didn't tell her," "the Vamp" (later to evolve into "the Other Woman"). Actors built firm careers playing the same type in every movie they made. Eventually, star actors were known by some part of their anatomy: "The Back" (Marie McDonald) or "The Girl with the Million Dollar Legs" (Betty Grable). The moviegoing public copied the fashions and hairdos of the stars and voraciously read magazine articles on their lives. In these diverse ways the authority of the screen image exerted its control of the spectator's perception.

Acting in a silent film asked for a totally different set of techniques from acting either on stage or in a "talkie." The director gave instructions to the actors as the cameras were rolling, and could also call out encouraging remarks when an actor pleased him with some gesture or reaction. This latter directorial technique was helpful to the actor and director because it kept alive a link between the actor and his audience. The director served as a collective voice. Music was often used to get the actor into the mood of a serious or sentimental scene. A piano, cello, and violin would orchestrate the tempo and rhythms of the ebb and flow of emotion for the actor. John Ford at a later date would have an accordionist play softly, if the actors seemed to need or want help with the setting of the mood. Since no sound was being recorded, actors could improvise the scenes after the director explained what should happen in the scene. This improvisational quality in silent films does lend verisimilitude and tones down the exaggerated facial expressions. The use of music was not an entirely novel directorial device; Stanislavsky had used music and metronomes in his work with actors at the Moscow Art Theatre. Nor is the use of music a dated device; modern film directors like Steven Spielberg and George Lucas use it to aid the actors. Emotions follow an inner rhythm which changes according to the development of the action. Various intentions or objectives which the actor plays are analogous

D. W. Griffith during the early silent-movie period uses a megaphone to direct the action.

to the various themes in a musical composition.

In early silent comedies, improvisational skills were a basic requirement for the actor's technique. Every comic actor had to be ready *at a moment's notice* to begin playing a situation. On one occasion Mack Sennett used a passing Shriners' parade as an "instant location" for a film. Actors scurried to department stores for props; a stock character—a poor working girl looking for the father of her child—was assigned to Mabel Normand. Carrying a swaddled doll in her arms, Normand interrupted the line of parading Shriners, and Sennett filmed whatever reactions arose. "Something," Sennett said, "you couldn't have caught on film after six days of D.W. Griffith's rehearsals." The police arrived and chased the actors away, while Sennett filmed it all, added studio shots of close-ups and other scenes later to tie the story together; and thus another Sennett comedy was finished.

Improvisational techniques, the use of music and non-actors, scene rehearsals and the inclinations of the audiences to give identities to film "presences," continue to be mainstays of filmmaking in America and across the globe as well.

Although acting styles changed over the years, always seeking to be more realistic, the success of refining the filmmaking art depended on the changing expectations of the audience, the conventions in use in the theatre, and on the experimentations of film directors. In Russia, Sergei Eisenstein and Vsevolod Pudovkin, for instance, used in their montages brief shots of fixed expression on actors' faces, yet both directors rehearsed the actors in longer improvisations to stimulate the emotions. In an interview in *Experimental Cinema*, another talented Russian filmmaker, Alexander Dovzhenko, described his method of work: "to force a non-actor to make a certain grimace or movement. To *provoke* him to do it. For instance, a scene requires astonishment;—then, to provoke in him the expression of this astonishment by the aid of the feats of a skillful juggler." Filmmakers then and now have always tried to catch the actor by surprise, to help him break out of any comfortable and habitual reactions. Ford used music, Sennett passing parades, and Dovzhenko brought in circus acts.

Hollywood businessmen were most skillful, though, at developing types which fulfilled the audience's expectations for their "dream people." Faces, voices, and mannerisms each became embodiments of images for the filmgoer. Film stars did not have to be trained actors if the embodiment of some characteristic became transformed into an image which appealed to the spectators. The attractive image spanning nine feet of screen could sell a lot of tickets. Businessmen in Hollywood made fortunes on the selling of one aspect of the actor's physical personality.

Film technicians, too, were quickly learning the tricks of the trade—changing stories through editing, and making, as cameraman Hal Mohr relates, "the heavy the leading man" in cases where the leading actor was not very good. Under the constant gaze of cameramen and editors, faces were dissected with awesome precision, while actors frankly analyzed their own features as artists might evaluate the depth and contours of their sculptures. Mary Pickford supposedly felt her face had only one photogenic side and managed to maneuver the camera's position to favor that side. If the continuity of the scene required her to turn in a direction she considered unflattering to her face, she would follow the continuity of the action with her eyes only, keeping her best side to the cameras.

Since then, countless stories of short men whose leading ladies had to stand in holes for the love scenes, and of maturing actresses who insisted upon being photographed behind scrims to soften the age lines have been as much a part of film acting as the plastic strip itself. In contrast to the theatre—where realism was triumphing, holding to an artistic creed to depict life with complete and objective honesty, valuing concrete, verifiable details—film art in its unrelenting examination of facial and body features brought the moviemaker's consciousness to an attentive posture of facial-shaping and illusion-making. Unlike the theatre realist who sought to avoid the romantic prettifying of his subjects, the film illusionists strived to create idealistic figures and new idols.

Through filmmaking and moviegoing, a new ritual was established which captured the imagination and hopes of audiences throughout the world. The cinematic ritual encompassed the empathic relationship of actors and directors, the often symbiotic relationship of businessman and artist, and the sometimes strict canonical relationship of the acolyte-spectator and the idolized star. The ritual became a release for the societal pressures of the time, and visualized in its actors and actresses and in its subject matter of filmed stories the aspirations, the depressions, and in rare moments, the lustre of the natural world.

Directors of vision inspired actors of sensibility to regard them as "gods" for whom they would risk their lives—as Lillian Gish did on the ice floe in Griffith's film, *Way Down East*. The artists of silent film had constantly to collide with the "barkers" of the business, the producers and the movie-theatre owners. Audiences required their idols to remain constant in their magic.

The spectrum of these new "shamans" was wide: William S. Hart, Pearl White, Charlie Chaplin, the Keystone Cops and Bathing Beauties, Erich Von Stroheim, Bessie Love, and Sally O'Neil. Never since have there been so many beloved clowns— Laurel and Hardy, "Fatty" Arbuckle, Harry Langdon, Buster Keaton, and Chester Conklin. In film, even the shoes of Charlie Chaplin became stars. They were used to advertise his films. Only in film can objects take on personality and convey in one glance as much as any expression on an actor's face. Thus a new art was delivered, a kind of tribal ritual with its own witch doctors performing in a darkened room, leading the spectator to enter a condition of repose, of half-sleep awaiting that state of dream Shakespeare described in *A Midsummer Night's Dream:*

> And sleep, that sometime shuts up sorrow's eye,
> Steal me awhile from mine own company.

Can there be, then, such an art as film acting? Can anyone "act" on film at all? Is the face or body of a film identity another tool in the hands of the major collaborators—the director, designers, musicians? And are they all in the hands of the cameramen?

There is a classic example of the dilemma of filmmaking art in Soviet filmmaker Lev Kuleshov's classroom experiment. He showed his audience footage of an expressionless man intercut with footage of food, a corpse, and a girl. All in the room associated feelings of hunger, grief, and love with the man. Can we say, then, that the man is "acting", since the director had told the man to do absolutely nothing with his face, and since the man had been completely ignorant of what shots would follow, making him unable to develop a relationship to those objects? Isn't he rather part of a montage, a creative idea formed through the use of juxtaposed images on celluloid? Many film actors and directors today believe that to do nothing is usually effective on camera.

Way Down East. *Location shooting often challenged the actor's stamina and courage.*

Is there a place in filmmaking for the actor to analyze the facets of character and amalgamate those with his own individuality? In an interview by film critic Ronald Hayman, Italian director Michelangelo Antonioni states that analysis is not necessary:

> . . . the film actor need not understand, but simply be. One might reason that in order to be, it is necessary to understand. That's not so. If it were, then the most intelligent actor would also be the best actor. Reality often indicates the opposite. When an actor is intelligent, his efforts to be a good actor are three times as great, for he wishes to deepen his understanding, to take everything into account, to include subtleties, and in doing so he trespasses on ground which is not his . . . in fact, he creates obstacles for himself. His reflections on the character he is playing, which according to popular theory should bring him closer to an exact characterization, end up by thwarting his efforts and depriving him of naturalness. The film actor should arrive for shooting in a state of virginity. The more intuitive his work, the more spontaneous it will be.

Antonioni's argument is a semantic jubilee of words, which can be interpreted in as many ways as there are actors capable of doing so. The actor may well create obstacles for himself for many and varied reasons, the least of which is due to his efforts to include subtleties or deepen his understanding. The actor's insecurities may block or scatter his energies. An actor needs channel markers to chart his way through a characterization which must be repeated for several takes. These markers may be as simple as a decision to empty himself, as well as more complex decisions to try different ways of affecting the other actors.

The technique of shooting many takes, an essential feature of film acting, creates obstacles for keeping the actor's intuitive capability engaged. Intuitive playing is easiest on the first take. By the second one, all sorts of complicated energies are working on the actor. He may find it hard to ignore the responsibility he feels to do a good job on each take. He may be burdened by the weight he ascribes to the consequences of his actions during any take. These kinds of thoughts are not a result of any particular degree of intelligence. They are provoked by the emotional relationship of the actor to himself, his talent, and his ability to do the work. Intuition is crucial to film acting, but the actor must be able to keep it working in a free manner.

Intuition is a capacity of the intellect which blends disparate impressions into a ready apprehension of idea, emotion, or situation. Its sister muse is imagination. Intuition does not spring fully gowned from a woman's breast, as some filmmakers believe. Nor does it make a debut at some magic age in either men or women. It is developed through repeated experiences of remaining vulnerable to life and activity, whether animal, vegetable, or mineral. The intellectual analysis of a script does not inhibit intuition, just as analyzing life experiences does not preclude a sensitivity to them. Socrates' belief that "the unexamined life is not worth living" applies to art as well. The unexamined art is not worth doing. Examination cannot cut off intuition unless the examiner gives it that power.

Marlon Brando, Vanessa Redgrave, Jane Fonda, George C. Scott, Joanne Woodward, Donald Sutherland, and others like them are intuitive actors, yet they are also capable of the intellectual analysis of a script and its meaning. Their films reveal that in creating obstacles for either themselves or the director (as the case may be), these actors will often find original and imaginative character action for the scene.

Antonioni's films are often wonderfully convoluted in intellectual mind-bending and -breaking; his films often use faces and bodies to embody ideas. Both Brando and Antonioni make exciting films. Both methods of work seem to depend on the personal orientation of each artist to the world around him. In Brando's case, "reflections on the character" certainly don't thwart his efforts or deprive his characterization of an organic naturalness. Antonioni seems most interested in using spontaneous personality traits of actors, then editing their film images to produce his ideological orientation. It strikes one as a kind of sculpture filmmaking. Any modification of a gesture or pose in editing will modify the image and construct the idea. Any skillful director or editor can create a star actor or an imaginative gestural sequence by splicing and cutting the film. Antonioni prefers to choose specific physical attitudes, movements, and gestures by casting certain actors or non-actors in his films whose physical mannerisms and personas will serve the idea. The trained actor sometimes feels like Rod Steiger, who has ruefully referred to an actor's being no more than a "can of peas" to be opened and used.

The organic suggestions of youth and middle-age by Fonda and Redgrave reflect their creative skill.

The nature of film and the many methods of work make it essential to realize the actor's contribution is also multifaceted. Much of the footage in a film is simple physical action: getting in and out of vehicles, riding horses across a prairie, looking up, down, or all around. The actor must perform these actions without embellishment. Part of the footage is montage in which the actor is simply one facet of several rhythmic elements that create impressions and ideas. In montage, the actor is required to perform whatever the director has envisioned for a particular pictorial composition (his unique contribution to the film). Fortunately, some of the work in film will relate to characterization, and it is in this area that the actor can contribute the finer elements of *his* skill and talent.

3

THE AESTHETIC NATURE OF FILM ACTING

Converting the intellect into passion

—Pirandello

PHYSICAL IMPACT AND KINESTHETIC APPEAL

If we are to understand what the film actor can do, then we must first understand something of the nature of the film medium itself. The first quality that must be comprehended is that film is spectacularly *physical*. It is the accumulation of physical images which moves the audience to become involved. Unlike the novel, there are no pages to be filled; there is a rectangular screen to be filled with physical images. Film direction is often compared to the art of musical composition. A composer places "little black notes" —as Alfred Hitchcock called them—on a piece of paper. Out of these notes we get music. Similarly, on the screen a director places images. Out of these we get story and character.

This physical element overrides all other considerations for the creation of the image of character. In her book *Unholy Fools*, Penelope Gilliatt says, "The weight that cinema gives to sensuous

Eli Wallach and Carroll Baker in Baby Doll. *The still photograph evokes the relationship, character, and narrative elements through the manner of embraces, facial expressions, and props (Coke bottles, movie magazines, the crib), and through the physical juxtaposition of the two figures.*

detail is one of its greatest potencies, distinguishing it sharply from the theatre." What is sensuous detail?

Certainly this does not simply mean sexual appeal, nor is it glamorous or peculiar features. Rather it is the combination of all elements perceived through the senses: type and color of the skin and eyes; contours of the nose; musculature of the face and body; rhythms of the walk and any bodily movement; kinetics (the study of the relationship of motion and the forces affecting motion); and, probably most important, kinesthesia (the sensation of bodily position, presence, or movement resulting chiefly from stimulation of sensory nerve endings).

In simpler terms, what does this mean? That John Wayne's stride, Jack Benny's mincing walk, Marilyn Monroe's rolling, roiling glide, Jack Nicholson's grin, Al Pacino's hooded eyes, Madeline Kahn's round eyes, or Goldie Hawn's mobile lips and mouth, communicate to us as viewers far more than mere physical configuration or motion. The physical image evokes a response from us, a response of kinship. The associations we attach to the physical configurations or motions spring from our memories, our emotional experiences, our perceptions of objects and ideas. The physical image presents itself, and we imbue it with meaning.

Underneath the motion of the actor, there is the powerful communication of magnetism. We are drawn through the motion into a personal "presence" that has evolved within the actor since childhood, one that is unconscious, spontaneous, and tells us some facts about the person which we could garner no other way. Watch, for instance, two adolescents on a college campus speaking to each other. The girl may hold her books tightly against her chest, perhaps shifting occasionally from one foot to the other. The young boy stands with pelvis thrust forward, hands on hips. It is a physical language, and conveys better than words what is happening between the two young people who themselves are only consciously aware of doing no more than discussing yesterday's assignment.

In Hal Ashby's film *Being There*, Shirley MacLaine (as Eve Rand) visits Peter Sellers (playing Chance Gardiner) for a morning chat. She sits on the bed next to him. Gently passing the tips of her fingers over her neck area, she looks at Gardiner, then at the television show he's watching, then looks back at him. The manner in which she executes these motions—the timing and the rhythm

—and the way she handles her peignoir and arranges herself on the side of the bed make a complex impact on us. The information we receive from her physical choices of movement is that her slow and graceful external motion covers a churning desperation to embrace him.

Film communicates vividly the physical and the kinesthetic. The aesthetic weight of the actor, his physical emphasis, influences our perception of his screen presence. We see not only his particular features, but we also perceive his life rhythms, his unique kinetic and kinesthetic response to living things and persons, his "way of being" as Ingmar Bergman terms it. As we watch the actor perform, our first information based on his external physical characteristics is altered and deepened through his vocal intonation, his speech rhythms, his conscious and unconscious mannerisms, his own self-image.

Charles Bronson is a strong screen presence because his face, especially his eyes and mouth, immediately communicate the quiet but violent killer type. We make judgments about the "kind of person" the actor is, just as we make judgments about people we've observed waiting in an airport terminal or behind a sales counter. Film is the first medium to offer us in such detail this opportunity to respond to an artist the way we respond to the people we see and deal with every day.

The giant size of the image in a movie theatre sharpens our emotional responses and perception of the image, acting upon us as images within our dreams do, on an unconscious as well as a conscious level. We learn in our daily encounters how to read the faces of those around us, starting in childhood when we cope with and learn to trust another "giant-size" image—the parent's face looking into the crib from above. This reading or interpretation of physical facts is based on subtle movements and changes in the face, particularly those involving the muscles surrounding the eyes and mouth. We read into those changes any number of various motivations, intentions, and thoughts. We interpret the text beneath the surface movement. In film we can linger much longer on the immense "movie face" and have little difficulty seeing and responding to the smallest and subtlest of changes, and determining what lies beneath the shifts in motion. Each of us, to some extent based on our experiences, will make judgments.

The film actor must be aware, then, that anything that intrudes in the projection of emotion will be vividly conveyed: the mannerisms of the actor, the slightest suggestion of unrelated thought, self-consciousness, self-direction, or fatigue. Any unrelated motion will be communicated as part of the scene.

Faye Dunaway's performance in *Chinatown* faltered for some of these reasons. What was perceived within the character was Dunaway's calculations and criticisms of her characterization: a silent message of "This should certainly be a forties' look" or "Isn't this like Joan Crawford's poker-face expression?" We have no way of knowing whether this is a flaw in the actor's technique or the outcome of a conflicting relationship with a director whose brand of critical remarks forces the actor into self-conscious behavior. Even the choice of makeup for Dunaway's character in the movie was overstated and excessively stylized. This in itself would encourage the actor to play a parody of the era. As the actor sits at the makeup table and observes the changes in hairstyle and the cosmetic emphasis of certain features, she begins slowly to take on the characteristics of the character, the persona she witnesses emerging from the mirror image. Perhaps director Roman Polanski, captivated by the makeup, or infatuated by a star of the forties, became a modern Pygmalion who carved a statue of *his* ideal vision, but allowed no Aphrodite to release Dunaway to develop a living character.

Contrast Dunaway's portrayal in *Chinatown* with Maggie Smith's performances in *Travels with My Aunt* and *Death on the Nile*. Smith absorbs all the stylization of costume and manners, converting it into an extension of personality. She uses the costume to develop organic behavior. Perhaps the best example of adapting stylization to organic behavior can be found in Maggie Smith's portrayal of Jean Brodie in *The Prime of Miss Jean Brodie*. The accent, the theatrical mannerisms, the zest for creating beauty distinguished Smith's flamboyant performance, yet created a unique and credible individual. Actors must wear costume and makeup like a second skin.

Jane Fonda's performances in *They Shoot Horses, Don't They?* and *Julia* project a similar identification with the style of the periods in the two films. Fonda appears "at home" in the garb of the period, making it work for the characterization, letting it influence

Faye Dunaway in Chinatown. *Since this film Dunaway's performances have become excessively stylized, leading to a near-caricature performance in* Mommie Dearest.

her behavior. Dunaway's mannerisms in *Chinatown* seem a superficial veneer with little solid characterization beneath them. As Joan Crawford in the film based on Christina Crawford's book, *Mommie Dearest*, Dunaway uses to advantage her particular physical characteristics: cold eyes and a cool, chic demeanor.

Whatever form an actor's self-consciousness or self-containment takes will be projected alongside his image of character. An actor's self-awareness must include being careful of one's own refinement and public image, not letting it show through as an element with its own life. This is a difficult hurdle to overcome not only in the actor's art of telling the truth on screen but also in all art; for as Iris Murdoch commented in *The Black Prince*, "how almost impossibly difficult it is not to let the marvels of the instrument itself interfere with the task to which it is dedicated."

Dunaway's most effective movie characterization was the Bonnie she developed under Arthur Penn's direction in *Bonnie and Clyde*. By playing down and playing against the beauty of Dunaway's features, and the starkness of her presence, Penn and Dunaway pulled the viewer inside the truth—the bitterness and amorality of the character.

Techniques of the legitimate theatre often become like 8 x 10 glossy photos—smoothly finished copies of an original expression that worked. Film techniques more easily become self-imitations or packaged images for the publicity departments. In an interview in *Directors in Action*, John Cassavetes warned, "You have to fight sophistication. Sophistication comes to anybody who has been doing his job for awhile. You have to fight knowing, because once you know something, it's hard to be open and creative; it's a form of passivity—something to guard against." In film, passivity will be *actively* communicated, so great is the weight of the physical. We can be mesmerized by misleading conceptions, totally foreign to what the director or actor wished to convey within the scene.

The film actor should try to retain as much curiosity about what's going to happen in the story as the character does. Marcello Mastroianni believes that while the director should study the script, the actor should not. Mastroianni prefers that the actor remain "available" to the event—like a child's availability to a game of make-believe. In children's games, each child is assigned a part. Instantly the child's willingness to become another character blossoms into improvisation and play, with no self-criticism.

Intellectual judgments made by the actor, split-second hesitations which obstruct free play by the emotions, or any physical, mental, or emotional movement by the actor will color his image of character and muddy the waters of understanding in the interpretation by the audience.

Before the actor can begin work on the character, he must understand the necessity in film for believability (truth in the doing), develop a self-awareness unflawed by misleading messages or sophisticated, meaningless action, and comprehend the dynamic effect of juxtaposed images, and the potency of the physical in film. As Stanislavsky noted, the physical includes the inner actions of the mind and emotions as well as the external physical actions.

Actors like Brando, Max Von Sydow, Jane Fonda, Dustin Hoffman, Robert Redford, Robert De Niro, Joanne Woodward, and Rosemary Harris, who devote their careers to a study and refinement of their film techniques, are like composers of études, whose work seen collectively will seem the counterpointed melodies of symphonies. Robert Duvall has already created a body of work that is impressive in its breadth and depth. From characterizations such as Boo Radley in *To Kill a Mockingbird* to the flamboyant warrior without a war in *The Great Santini*, Duvall has worked to develop believable, complex people on the screen.

CATEGORIES OF ACTING TYPES IN FILM

Film acting is not in any way, though, limited to these acting musician-auteurs. The power that the camera has to project sensual matter and energy gives rise to a phenomenon involving actors that does not occur in the legitimate theatre. In film anyone can act. Any person found anywhere placed in the right part will create a character on film. In the theatre the actor must be able to project his voice to fill whatever space there is. He must be able to be understood. He must be able to play someone other than himself if he is to be acknowledged as a successful stage actor. Not so in film. Because film does exert a gravitational force on our perception equal to the sensual, physical mass of the person or objects we see, we more readily accept various types as film "actors."

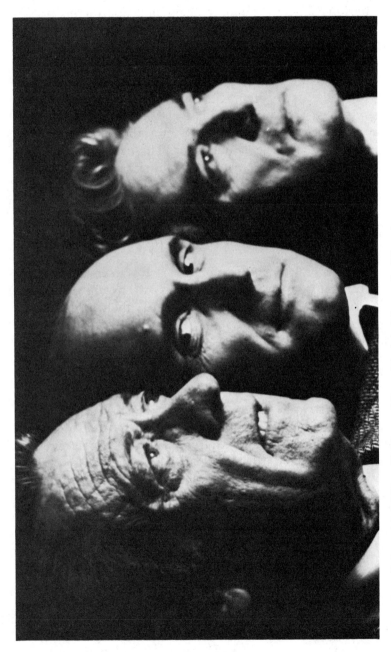

Robert Duvall (c.) with William Holden and Peter Finch in Network. There is always an element of unpredictability in Duvall's characterizations.

This ready perception and acceptance is both a blessing and a curse: a blessing, because it allows the use of people on the street; a curse because the dedicated actor who wishes to create varied characters must cope with the ability of the camera to give his presence a "name."

In film there are various categories of actors, categories based on the type and style of gravitational force exerted upon the viewers' psyches. We can divide these classifications of film types into four simplified areas: the character actor; the personality actor; the physical actor; and the natural actor. These divisions will help us understand the aesthetic nature of film art; the boundaries of each division may be crossed by many fine actors.

The Character Actor

The character actor is the actor who strives to create an image of character that is an amalgamation of his own psyche and that of the written image. Character actors can purify their own personas and cloak them with new personas that are whole, natural, and grounded in reality. The spectator, though aware of the actor, responds to this new image of character, forgetting for the time the actor himself. You no longer think of Laurence Olivier, you see Archie Rice in *The Entertainer*. Dustin Hoffman's Ratso in John Schlesinger's *Midnight Cowboy* is a brilliant transformation of actor into character. Hoffman's choice of physical details for each character he plays is original and inventive. Ratso is a good-hearted, slightly backward individual. The walk, the manner of speaking, and the degree of emotional trust in others are all distinctive choices in Hoffman's portrayal.

In Sam Peckinpah's *Straw Dogs*, Hoffman creates a selfish, cold but polite man who changes into a savage defender of his home. In *Agatha*, Hoffman does not succeed as well in absorbing the physical manifestations he selected for the character of Wally Stanton, except in isolated instances. More often than most actors, though, Hoffman attempts to create a new persona for each character he plays.

The blend of the two—the actor and the image—is subtle. You are not aware where one ends and the other begins, or which part of the mode of emotional approach is the actor's and which the character's. It is not a Halloween disguise of costume and makeup. It is an inner change of approach to others, of methods of communicating self, both internally and externally. It is a change in the core of activity, whether mental or emotional, out of which the character responds to the world around him.

At times the internal stretch for the actor is a small one (permitting the actor to behave as spontaneously as he himself would in the same circumstances). At other times, the stretch may be large, requiring the actor to submerge his own responses and take on new ones. The great actor never seems to reveal how large the stretch is.

Joanne Woodward and Estelle Parsons in *Rachel, Rachel*; Marlon Brando in *The Ugly American*, *Last Tango in Paris*, and *The Formula*; Jane Fonda in *Klute* and *Julia*; Donald Sutherland in *Ordinary People, Don't Look Now, Casanova*, and *The Eagle Has Landed*; Dustin Hoffman in *Midnight Cowboy* and *Agatha*, succeeded in keeping their own personal mannerisms hidden, subjecting them either to new mannerisms, or by dynamically giving themselves over to a different internal approach to others. For example, Woodward's way of walking as Rachel incorporated slumped shoulders, the abdomen carried forward, and the knees turned inward. In *The Entertainer*, Olivier covered a seedy insecurity with a zestful "hail-fellow-well-met" cheeriness. Hoffman used a half-smile, half-sneer as he dealt with various establishments. Sutherland almost always changes drastically his physical appearance for his roles, and absorbs the external changes to create an internal appearance as well, one that matches the outer appearance.

We find a common denominator in many of these successful characterizations: layered over the duality of the actor "being" and "acting," we witness simultaneously a duality in the character itself. As we respond to the false joviality of Archie Rice, we are also conscious in that moment of his depressive insecurity. A twinge of sympathy passes through our response to Archie Rice's flamboyance. Duality created by the actor produces a duality of response in the spectator. The complexity of this inner action in both the actor-character and the spectator accounts in some part for our fascination with character actors, and nourishes our desire to see them in role after role.

Laurence Olivier as vaudeville comedian Archie Rice in The Entertainer.

The Personality Actor

A second category of acting types has developed out of the physical potency of film and the aesthetic weight of the person involved. In a famous paper on acting, the French actor Louis Jouvet describes this aesthetic weight: "Every human being has a specific gravity. Before an audience one may say that the comedian has a density—the quality of his presence. The comedian must learn to make use of this dynamism, this kind of aura that surrounds him." In the tradition of French theatre, the term "comedian" means an actor who can play all roles, rather than one who distorts the role to fit his personality.

Just as a painting through form, composition, color, and texture evokes a response in the viewer, so does the physical presence of an actor. This individual, unique physical presence or aura is developed through childhood, and is in part molded through education and experience. It contains threads of motion and inner activity that reach back through generations. It combines intelligence, physical features, and vulnerability. Part is myth, part is mystery, part is fact. The aura is the weight of the soul communicated through a particular physical framework.

In film the camera makes use of this dynamism, as Jouvet calls it, whether or not the actor does, or whether or not the actor is even aware of the quality and density of his presence. Charles Bronson is aware of his camera presence, and chooses roles to include the sinister, slit-eyed aura of a disengaged but dangerous man—the composition and texture of his film presence. The wizardry of the camera produces this phenomenon of giving identity to the physical characteristics.

The face, the mannerisms, the aura of anyone on film can develop a life separate from the person or the actor. The face becomes in one sense an identifiable persona, which may or may not coincide with the actor's offscreen identity. The personality, in combination with the physical characteristics and personal mannerisms, are so vivid, so striking that the "name" of the actor-person is identified as the "persona" by the audience. This aura may also be strengthened by the actor's sense of authority and self-sufficiency.

In the 1940s Ma and Pa Kettle films, Percy Kilbride's self-sufficiency arose from his seeming totally at ease and forever at home as the henpecked husband of Marjorie Main. Percy Kilbride in any role would seem to be "Gabby Hayes." This phenomenon produces what we term the personality actor. Spencer Tracy, Marlene Dietrich, Gary Cooper, Burt Lancaster, Kirk Douglas, James Stewart, and Katharine Hepburn; Joan Crawford, John Wayne, Peter Lorre, Bette Davis, Humphrey Bogart, and Sidney Greenstreet, become personality actors because of this phenomenon. Each name is an identity which is immediately responded to as a *character* by the audience. Think, for instance, of Spencer Tracy at *Bad Day at Black Rock* or Gary Cooper in *High Noon*. The actor-person *is* the character.

In many performances of personality actors, the range of emotion covers only a few notes of the actor's instrument. We see the same octave replayed in various environments, in diverse conflicts, in a series of time periods. The costumes, makeup, settings, and circumstances change, but the character and its responses remain the same in depth and complexity. Some critics would still claim these superstars are not actors.

In the essentially imagistic world of film every face and the peculiar musical note it resonates must be termed "actor." These personality actors cannot be held responsible for a condition the nature and power of film imposes upon their presences. They are still required to fulfill certain expectations any actor must give his audience: that is, the actions must be performed believably. They are not able to create a character other than the one that is developed by the camera's image-making power, but they are able to progress through a series of emotional developments that are genuine and organic. Sometimes the latter does not occur.

We need only to recall the disaster of acting in *The List of Adrian Messinger*, in which a number of personality actors put on false noses, plastic cheeks, chins, and foreheads in a mistaken effort at transforming themselves, to see the inability of many personality actors to play a wide spectrum of roles. The main character in that movie was the unseen makeup artist who played the game with the audience of "Guess who's under all this putty?" Yet Frank Sinatra, disguised as a gypsy trader in that film and frozen there in a false face, has done some excellent acting within the range of his octave of emotional experience in films like *From Here to Eternity*, *The Manchurian Candidate*, and *The First Deadly Sin*.

Percy Kilbride and Marjorie Main in Ma and Pa Kettle Go to Town. *An example of actors who became identified with the roles they played.*

Marlene Dietrich and John Wayne in Pittsburgh. The cast in her left eye gives Dietrich a mysterious sensuality.

Sinatra's aura, aesthetic weight, and personal magnetism evoke a feeling of childlike vulnerability and sadness, sensitizing the spectator to that same vulnerability within himself. Sinatra was perfectly cast in those films which allowed the camera to explore the sensibility and openness which lay very near the surface of his skin. Fred Astaire's performance in *On the Beach* accomplished the same success of surprising depth.

Since film itself gives such super-significance to the dynamic aura of these person-actors, it places a tough obstacle in the way of their attempting characterization. Most personality actors do not attempt to play other than their screen personas; many could not play other. This limitation, partially imposed by the spectator, certainly should not disqualify them as actors. It illustrates the interconnection between the aura of any person on screen and the spectator. It is a unique partnership.

There is a world of experience written on each of the personality actors' faces, and the moviegoer requires that certain personas he has identified remain the same from movie to movie. Movie actors people the spectator's world; they are more real to him than theatre actors. The nature of film in its projection of an immense image in a darkened theatre accounts for this relationship of actor and spectator.

Crossing the borderline between character acting and personality acting requires the actor to find the role which allows him to make the passage. Jane Fonda, who began her film career as a typical personality starlet, developed into a character actor through her roles in *They Shoot Horses, Don't They?*, *Klute*, and *Julia*. The passage begins when the actor finds roles that suit her own set of mannerisms and personality mechanisms, and then goes on to create new mechanisms for the next role.

The personality actor may be developed and limited by the identification of the actor with a certain personality type, or in a particular role, as illustrated by the cases of Percy Kilbride in the Pa Kettle role, or Gabby Hayes as a crusty, old Western hand, or Zasu Pitts as a scatter-brained wreck. In other cases, such as those of John Wayne, Humphrey Bogart, or Peter Lorre, the individual physical and personality characteristics of the actor make such a strong statement that it is almost impossible for the spectator to accept the submersion of that personality in any role.

The Physical Actor

The third type of film actor is the physical actor. This is one who embodies either a "type" that is presently in vogue with the general population as an ideal, such as Ali McGraw, Bo Derek, or Brooke Shields, or one who possesses a particular physicality that is in some way excessive or extraordinary, such as Marty Feldman or Raquel Welch. It is characteristic in these instances that the physicality is exploited in every role. One of Welch's films is titled, for instance, *Mother, Jugs, and Speed*.

Watching these actors on film, we sometimes cringe at their lack of ability to perform actions or even say words in a believable way. Even their gestures are limited. Bo Derek's "character action" consisted of putting her finger to her teeth and opening her eyes a little wider in *Tarzan, the Ape Man*. We accept these physical actors because we like to look at them. In life it is tactless to stare unabashedly at a beautiful woman or a handsome man. In film we are encouraged to do so uninhibitedly. These actors reflect a masculine ideal and sentimental view of beauty, sexuality, villainy, or innocence.

Bo Derek, Tab Hunter, George Hamilton, Raquel Welch, Marilyn Monroe, and Elizabeth Taylor are breathing visual images of beauty. Monroe and Taylor are, of course, more than just physical actors. Taylor, in particular, in *Who's Afraid of Virginia Woolf?* gave one of the best performances of characterization in screen history.

Some physical actors embody "types" such as the "girl next door" (Sandra Dee, Doris Day, Debbie Reynolds); some the "sex-kitten" or "tiger" (Brigitte Bardot, Jane Russell, Suzanne Somers, and Raquel Welch). Although their bodies are always present on film, they often appear dissociated from the events which are taking place. Some, like Taylor and Monroe, are less self-conscious about their features. Monroe's sensuality was also associated with a sense of irony on her part. She seemed to be communicating, "I know what you're thinking; and I'm thinking it, too. Aren't we all fools, and isn't it fun?" Welch, on the other hand, seems to advertise her availability. In part, Welch has been marketed for this kind of appeal. Her most successful film acting was in *Kansas City Bomber*, which explored the raw-edged violence of competition, a quality which Welch embodies better than most physical actors.

It is evident that the right role, then, will allow any of these categories of actors to create images of character. Monroe, in *Bus Stop* and *The Misfits*, and George Hamilton, in *Evel Knievel*, *Love at First Bite*, and *Zorro, the Gay Blade*, found in roles qualities of character superbly matched to the aura and aesthetic weights of their personalities. The character images in these films also required a strong focus on physical attributes. Even the title, *The Misfits*, suits the aspect of Monroe as the child in the sensual body.

The Natural Actor

The fourth category of film actor is the natural. This is usually a person found by the director "off the street." Although the personality of the individual is not so magnetic as to develop an identity of its own, it is an individualistic identity superbly embodied in appropriate physical characteristics, and reflecting an enormous subtext of emotion beneath the physical. Federico Fellini has made imaginative use of people he has found in his shooting environments, finding them, as he said in an interview in the *New York Times*, "frequently more professional than professionals . . . sometimes professional actors are too rigid in their specialty to suit my purposes." The "specialty" Fellini refers to can be type—the intellectual; quality—vitality or pathos; or it can be either type or quality.

Observing these naturals in Fellini's movies, one must agree that it would be extremely difficult for any actor to don costume and makeup and convey character as vividly as those Fellini casts from the street. Sutherland is one actor who did accomplish this in his performance in Fellini's *Casanova*. The faces of the natural actors reflect a lifetime of experience—truth, fate, or experience is incorporated into the structure, in the lines and wrinkles, in the configuration of the face. There is no division of actor-person. The person is the actor. Successful acting for the natural actor depends only on the director's keeping him in an unself-conscious state. Fellini more than any other director has made the most creative collaborative use of the camera's physical potential in casting the roles in his films. His films come closest to poetry in their exploration of the truth, beauty, pity, and terror of the human condition, partially because the faces of the people in his films are strong visual metaphors of those elements, and Fellini knows the right location and context in which to place them.

The scene in *Amarcord* between the adolescent boy and the mammoth-breasted shopkeeper, in which she tries to teach him how to fondle her breast in sexual satisfaction, and the boy is surrounded by the massive pounds of flesh, not knowing in which direction to go, or what to do, is a masterpiece of comic sensuality.

These categories of film actors can only be loosely defined, because the boundaries are not so clearly set up that an actor from one category cannot cross over into another, given the proper role and director to guide him. Any actor interested in film work must be aware of his aesthetic weight or dynamism, must objectively know into which category he fits naturally, and whether or not he has the power to offset the identity film itself will contribute to his image.

We are hooked on the screen by the physical—the infant accessibility of Marilyn Monroe, the eyes of Liv Ullmann, the spacestar body of Raquel Welch, the nose of Barbra Streisand, just as earlier audiences were hooked by the "It" girl, Clara Bow, the smouldering glances of Theda Bara, the "c'mon and hit me, I'll love it" look of Gloria Grahame. The film actor must decide if he is able to submerge himself so thoroughly in a new set of mannerisms and physical characteristics that the camera will communicate this new identity as powerfully as his own personality. Dustin Hoffman succeeded in doing this in his characterization of Ratso in *Midnight Cowboy*, Donald Sutherland succeeded in *Casanova*, Jane Fonda in *Julia*. Perhaps successful transformation into character depends upon having a face that is mobile, but also somehow indistinct enough to take on new characteristics which project a distinctly different inner image of personality.

The personality actor, the physical, and the natural need only to remain in a relaxed, unself-conscious state before the camera, and perform the actions honestly and simply. Characterization and transformation are not necessary since character is already meshed and identified with either personality or physical characteristics. For these film actors, the main concern will be to keep from

A collection of "naturals" used by Fellini in Fellini Roma.

intruding upon the mechanics of the action, rather than to transform themselves into an "other." The goal is to be believable in the
situation, to convey a linkage to the situation on the screen. John
Ford put it succinctly in a direction he once gave to John Wayne,
"Cut the crap, and do the thing." The physical action as visual
image will convey the story. Physical types, naturals, and personality actors must not weaken the impact of the image by any
stiffness or awkwardness. In effect, they should allow the "natural
self" to remain open and unaffected.

Often it becomes the director's task to refocus these actors'
attentions and energies. Vittorio De Sica described his method of
working with naturals in an interview in *Sight and Sound*: "My
method . . . is simply to live with them for days, even for weeks on
end, until they treat me as a friend and forget all about 'acting.' My
experience as an actor helps me enormously to time the take and to
catch them just at the right moment." De Sica provides the acting
technique, his natural actors provide the visual images.

The personality actor should try to increase the range of his
octave of responses, to develop a receptiveness to the event, a spirit
of improvisation which will allow him to respond in an unplanned
way. It may not be essential to increase the range of the notes he
plays, if he can find ways to vary the melodies by deepening his
responses through exploring simultaneous indications of an inner
life and an external attitude toward it. It would be pleasant to have
opportunities on film for personality and physical actors to surprise
us with unexpected actions every now and then. Such surprises
and changes may not be accepted readily by the average moviegoer
who expects a cafeteria array of faces and bodies to attract him to
the theatre. They may regard any new behavior as a betrayal of the
unspoken pact between personality actor and spectator to have
things remain the same.

Lauren Bacall and John Wayne in *The Shootist* gave rich
performances that expanded our appreciation of their talents. Jack
Lemmon has taken advantage of several opportunities to deepen
our understanding of his range, most notably in *The China Syn-
drome*.

Movies are most interesting when they offer opportunities to
actors to expand and deepen the ranges nature or the audiences or
the starmakers have limited them to.

Film is a vast forest, offering space to many kinds of actors. The towering giants of character actors are not enough to satisfy our dream images. There must also be the fragrant blooms of personality actors, the undergrowth of unknown faces, as well as actors to represent the monsters and horrors of the caves of darkness.

4

THE ARTIST

THE PSYCHOPHYSICAL EXAMINATION

The psychophysical has received much attention and emphasis in acting schools during the past twenty years. Acting techniques at one time focused on the development of vocal and physical techniques, each one separate from the other. Actors learned phonetic diction, vocal support, and diaphragmatic breathing. Speeches were dissected and graphed for breathing pauses, particular words were selected for extra emphasis or stress. Physical techniques included posture refinement and exercises to develop graceful movement. The body and voice were trained to be instruments of ideal beauty: resonant diction from graceful bodies.

With the advent of Stanislavsky's work at the Moscow Art Theatre, this focus on external techniques was shifted to an internal technique. Stanislavsky labored to find means for the actor to have some control over what appeared to be inspired moments in acting—those moments when the actor unconsciously touched genuine emotions in himself and in the spectator.

As his work progressed, Stanislavsky discovered that by selecting and doing the right action for a particular circumstance, the correct emotion would be called up. This discovery is the beginning of the psychophysical technique in acting.

There are other threatre investigations which enhance the notion of the actor as a psychophysical artist: Delsarte's investigations of extroverted and introverted reactions; Meyerhold's biomechanical training; Oriental theatre techniques; and the discoveries made by Jerzy Grotowski in his work with actors.

The depth of response from Vivien Leigh and Marlon Brando engaging the total emotional and physical being in A Streetcar Named Desire *is possible only through vulnerability to the character and event.*

The psychophysical examination of an actor is an analysis of how well the actor's physical instrument reflects his psychological state. These two elements—the physical and the psychological—must work in tandem in order to accomplish a complete characterization. The examination tries to pinpoint for the actor what hinders him in the way of his respiration, his movement, and his degree of human contact. What must be identified are the actor's resistances to these elements. Once identified, these resistances can be eliminated, or at the very least, acknowledged by the actor.

Certain questions may be helpful to an actor to determine the degree of psychophysicality in his work:

- Does the actor find himself listening to the sound of his own voice during characterization? This attention indicates a separation in the psychophysical totality. The right side of the brain is acting as a critic, analyzing the method of delivery. The actor is attentive to the effect or result of his speech, rather than to achieving a goal through words.
- Does the actor appear to act from the neck up, disengaging the rest of his body from the action? This indicates a concentration on the cerebral characterization or verbal interpretation, and an inattention to the physical. Every actor must engage all the body in the activity of the character.
- Does the actor use more effort than is necessary to complete the action? Does he use more gestures than are necessary for simple emphasis? These kinds of dissipating physical activities are usually a sign of an excess of misdirected energy. They are an intrusion into characterization by the actor's fear of allowing the emotion or action to take charge or affect his whole physical being. Very often the actor will limit the emotion to one area of his body: the hands. But the hands are too fragile to contain all the forceful energy of emotion, and so they release it in tiny, numerous, and ultimately meaningless gestures. The larger muscles of the body must also be engaged. Exercises in using the whole body in active movement while rehearsing dialogue will retrain the actor. For example, the dialogue could be rehearsed while the actor is lifting large boxes and throwing them into another area. Even walking at a quick pace, or running in place while rehearsing the dialogue will engage the total musculature of the body in the action.

These exercises necessarily engage the larger muscles. The actor then can *experience* the physical feeling of having the whole body engaged, and more easily recreate that engagement without using an exercise. Retraining simply substitutes effective physical habits for ineffective ones.

Any mechanical emphasis on a single part of the actor's physiognomy indicates a break or gap in the psychophysical process. This gap may be linked to a tight jaw, a tendency to mumble, a shift in stance from foot to foot, clearing of the throat, excessive smiling, excessive movement of the lips, or nodding the head while listening. In all these circumstances, the actor has tried to contain the emotional power in one location, rather than allowing it to affect his total physical presence. It is the actor's way of controlling the emotion which makes him uncomfortable. It is important that the actor know why he is uncomfortable, and break through the barriers he has erected in human contact.

If the whole body is engaged in the action and emotional struggle, the characterization will be fluid, complete, and stimulating. The camera can help the actor in this self-analysis. Exercise scenes can be done in long, medium and close-up shots. The actor can then observe his behavior and ask others concerned with his development to comment on the behavior he projected through the camera's eye. Distracting mannerisms will be identified easily. More subtle withdrawals of the body from the action are more difficult to observe in one or two exercise scenes. More work with the camera on a regular basis will be necessary.

In order to succeed in a total self-revelation, the actor must try to eradicate the blocks in his behavior or action. Jerzy Grotowski's work with actors in his Polish Lab Theatre focuses on eliminating those elements of habitual behavior which mask pure impulse. Many of his techniques center on increasing the physical capabilities, thus tapping the single most important source of impulse.

All of our experiences are linked to physical sensations. We receive knowledge and experience events through our senses. This is a living fact; its dynamics act upon our behavior on a daily basis. It means, also, that we can make contact with original impulses through the bodily senses. People who have undergone Rolfing, for instance, often report a visual and experiential recreation of personal past events when certain areas of the body are manipulated. Work with the Alexander Technique has an amazing effect of releasing mental tension, emotional tightness, as well as relaxing physical tensions.

Experiences often teach us to hide behind certain physical or behavioral masks in order to cope with life events. The psychophysical examination is a technique of identification and elimination, when necessary, of these masks. A performance in film demands self-exposure.

VOICE

Clark Gable. Katharine Hepburn. Walter Brennan. Gary Cooper. Shelley Winters, James Stewart, Bette Davis. Jack Lemmon, Robert Mitchum, Woody Allen. Clint Eastwood, Walter Matthau, Kirk Douglas, Goldie Hawn. Shelley Duvall, Barbra Streisand, Jack Nicholson, Liza Minelli, Richard Pryor.

Each of these actors has a distinctive voice quality or speech pattern. These distinguishing vocal elements are a great part of the success these actors have had in films. Each voice contains an unusual characteristic, which defines a unique personality.

The film actor should not train his voice to sound like a stage actor using standard English pronunciation. He should preserve the quality of his voice and speech pattern, while learning to protect his voice from misuse or injury. The training and experience of radio and television announcers and reporters, for instance, gives them a specialized, disengaged vocal quality in which articulation and diction are emphasized. This kind of training would not be necessary for a film actor.

It is advantageous in film to have a distinctive voice quality and pattern, whether it be raspy, hesitant, thin, or resonant. The distinctive voice or speech pattern helps to establish the identity of an actor.

Other actors such as Vanessa Redgrave, Marsha Mason, Candice Bergen, Robert Redford, Ruby Dee, Paul Newman, Jill Clayburgh, James Caan, Burt Reynolds, Jane Fonda, and Sally Field have voices that resonate vulnerability and emotional empathy. These voices are pleasant sounding in pitch and variable in range.

In a perhaps apocryphal Hollywood story, it is said that John

Wayne's distinctive speech pattern of pausing after every two or three words, no matter how it affected the sense of a line, dismayed some directors, but delighted John Ford, who encouraged Wayne to retain this unusual characteristic in his speech pattern. Whatever the truth of that story, the point is that Wayne's speech pattern helped to create his tough but hesitant screen image.

In some of his early films, Humphrey Bogart used a stage diction and articulation which called attention to itself as a trained voice. Later in his career he relaxed and spoke more naturally, giving the screen one of its most fascinating voices.

Al Pacino, Robert De Niro, Dustin Hoffman, Stacy Keach, and others have the ability to change their voice and speech patterns for each role they play. Hoffman's Harry Stanton in *Agatha* speaks in a clipped monotone. This is admirable work from an actor, because the entire physical demeanor must also be changed to accommodate the new vocal pattern.

All film actors must be able to express vocally the nuances of feelings when the roles require, no matter what kind of natural voices they have. A voice like Shelley Duvall's is a disengaged voice. The thinness of the voice produces this effect of disengagement. In order for the spectator to believe that the actor with a disengaged voice is involved in the emotion of a scene, the actor must provide the voice with more resonant qualities and breath support during those scenes.

Breath control can be crucial to an actor, particularly in a "death" scene. Many times we have watched actors mourning the loss of their loved ones—other actors who lie there still obviously breathing. Breath-control exercises can be found in any vocal technique book. Every film actor would also benefit from singing lessons. Voice training increases both lung capacity in inhalation and control during exhalation.

One minor failing in film actors' breath control is an audible breath intake before each line of dialogue. Every few seconds there is a slight "huff" before the actor says the first words of a line. Often this is an unconscious habit that the actor can change quite easily once he recognizes the problem.

One of the technical jobs an actor has in a film is to loop additional dialogue, or lines. This may be a line that was not perfectly recorded by the sound technicians on the floor, or it may consist of offscreen lines that will be added to a shot. Occasionally, the actor may be required to loop entire scenes, even though they were recorded during shooting. The scene needing sound will be on a loop which runs through the projector again and again. This facilitates the actor's attempts to get the lines exactly synchronized, and with the emotional texture and meaning that he and the director want.

Many actors and sound technicians decry the extensive use of looping in films today. For some actors the increasingly prevalent attitude that one needn't worry about the sound of lines on the set promotes slackness and laziness. Historically, foreign films, especially those made in Spain and Italy, have always been dubbed or looped in a studio after the film has been shot. In these foreign films with a cast of many nationalities, the actors speak in their native languages when they shoot the scene. So dubbing or looping is an absolute essential. Imagine, though, the difficulty this presents for actors in timing cues. If your co-actor speaks Italian, and you don't, you will have a difficult time knowing when he is finished with his line, so that you can come in with yours.

Sound technicians complain that directors defer looping lines on a day-to-day basis; especially lines which they know have been garbled. These directors promise that it will be done the next day or in the post-production period. For many films, that day never comes. Indeed, it is noticeable that many recent films contain indistinct or hard-to-hear dialogue. Other complaints are that such unintelligible lines are let through in the post-production period, and that lines out of synchronation with the action are allowed to pass because the director thinks the shot looks good, and is willing to have less than perfect sound.

There are actors and directors such as Charlton Heston and Orson Welles who see looping as an additional opportunity to be more creative with a line reading. Looping for them offers a chance to try various readings of the lines. Readings which may add more subtle meaning to the lines can be experimented with during a looping session. An actor can experiment with various intentions and motivations on the lines. Different subtexts can be communicated with the words. As Charlton Heston has commented in his excellent journal of his acting career, *The Actor's Life. Journals 1956–1976*, "Even a dying scream has varying possibilities. ('Each man give me three deaths . . . two long, one short, please!')" This is the kind of professional attitude that can turn the chore of looping into a creative experience.

CINEMATIC ELEMENTS OF PERSONALITY

- The way you smile, after curling both lips in and maintaining them in that position until the instant you stop.
- The way you walk, the rhythm and weight of your step upon the ground.
- The way your eyes receive and reflect light.
- The degree of your muscle tension during stillness.
- The shape of your lips.
- The directness of your gaze.
- The almost imperceptible movement of your facial muscles when you whisper, speak softly, or shout.
- The tight and jutted jaw of your determined egoism.
- The hunched shoulders of your body when you are insecure.
- The downcast motion of your eyelids in reverie.

Personality resides in the physical. Innumerable changes in the musculature of the actor's body within his context of thought, emotion, or action create a physical home for personality. The two are so closely linked they are inseparable. A person who's ill doesn't "seem like herself." Why? The musculature motion we identify with her personality has changed because of sickness. She moves differently; she doesn't pay attention to others *in the same manner* as before. She is not "herself."

Though we each use two legs to stride, to saunter, to stroll, to tiptoe, we each make these motions in distinctive ways. Weight may be distributed in various ways on the two legs; the hips may be held in a certain way, or released in a certain way during the motion of walking. Even the upper torso and shoulders will be affected by the walk.

Although we each have two eyes which reflect light, each pair of eyes reflects light in varying degrees and intensities. Certain eyes

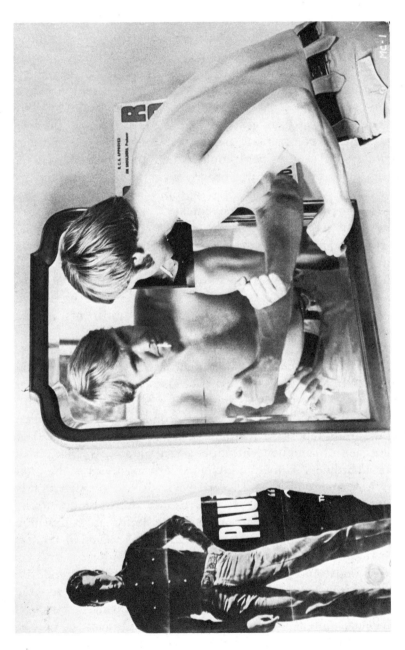

Jon Voight in Midnight Cowboy *cultivates a movie-inspired self-image.*

seem to be all light—Meg Foster's in *The Scarlet Letter*; others seem to be opaque—Fay Dunaway's in *Mommie Dearest*. The common tendency is to perceive light as openness, warmth, vulnerability; and to perceive opaqueness as coolness, secretiveness, and power.

In executing motion of any sort, we operate out of habits, some learned, some developed as protective devices, some accidental, some a result of a peculiar bodily strength or weakness. The eyes' reflective quality is a gift of nature. Expressiveness of the eyes is produced by contractions and relaxations within the muscles controlling the eyes. The Rudolf Laban theory of movement analyzes these as a complicated progression of basic and incomplete efforts made by the muscles. As the inner motion or intentions change and grow, these initial movements will involve more areas of the eyes: the eyelids, the eyebrows, the muscles controlling the nose, chin, and movements of these smaller parts of the body, parts that are usually in a state of repose.

All of our organic movements are a result of an orientation to living. We are each singularly expressive because we each have different past experiences, make different adjustments in the present, and hold different views on the future.

Personality is characterized by these physical manifestations. It is physical in the sense that all human acts, including the mental or emotional, are physical actions because of the psychophysical relationship. No action exists outside of a physical context. Any decision is the result of an inner action, conflict, or struggle. Even when we are in repose, or motionless, we are either moving out of one action or into another. Our inner activity is always reflected by the body. Stillness is not synonymous with inactivity of the total being. Movement of the inner powers, drives, or strivings is constant, though changing. It evolves, develops, refines itself, releases itself in movement or uses the body as a dynamic repository. Posture or stance is never static: it is a reflection of inner movement.

The body and facial structure of any individual and the quality of his or her motion communicates any number of variable attributes: warmth, coolness, accessibility, prudishness, recklessness, violence, intellectualism, mirth, naivete, calmness, complexity, and so on.

Walther Matthau on screen strikes one as a mirthful, adven-

Roy Scheider and Leland Palmer in All That Jazz.

turesome, unflappable spirit, a modern Puck. Why? Matthau has a very mobile face; his eyes are alert, sharp. He seems a friendly cynic, a wisecracking prankster. We never fear Matthau on screen. He's neither the epitome of somebody's favorite pal nor a raffish Lothario, but he does project some of these qualities, along with a childlike enthusiasm and sense of play. His body movement is relaxed and rather elegant. There is a looseness in his stride and in his speech. An easy, comforting geniality informs his motion. His naturalness communicates a lack of pretense in his outlook on human nature.

George C. Scott projects a solid, heavy, personal orientation to life. His movement is contained, fluid; fluid in the sense of heavy oil pouring into a cast iron container. His facial structure and movement project a sense of magnitude, a graceful severity marking his absolute concentration.

Katharine Hepburn casts sparks in the universe when she moves. Her angular facial structure conveys a brittle strength; her measured glances and speech mark an intelligence peppered with humor. The rhythm of her motion is that of an accomplished worker. Overall, these psychophysical elements are veiled with a sensitive femininity.

Film actors, great and small, project a physical individuality and personality which the camera aggressively communicates. Those film actors who wish to act characters must find the correct kinetic representation for the inner life of the character.

Laban, in his perceptive analysis, maintained several general categories of movement which can guide the actor in his selection of physical traits: pressing, thrusting, wringing, slashing, gliding, dabbing, flicking, and floating. These general descriptions of movement orientation can trigger the actor's imagination.

The actor might choose one of the types such as "pressing" for his basic mode of inner characterization. That is, the character will have a slow, steady, forceful mode of response to other characters and events. The actor may also use this image of "pressing" for the external characterization, or he may choose "gliding" for the external characterization. With the latter choice, a character would be more complex and less predictable. The inner character mode would be hard, while the external mode would be soft and more appealing.

Sophia Loren in Two Women. *The enclosed, self-protective body position accentuates the character's pain.*

The actor might use one of these motion types for a particular scene or shot. He might choose one which harmonizes with the mood of the character or scene, or one which is a counterpoint to the mood.

The cinematic and kinetic aspects of personality are distinguished by the manner in which an individual treats space, time, and weight. Character and temperament are often indicated by a struggle against or indulgence in these three elements. It is easy to conjure up images for a person who moves reluctantly and heavily through his space, as opposed to one who darts quickly and innocently through his space. George C. Scott and Simone Signoret move heavily through space, but with no sense of struggle against it. Dom De Luise and Sandy Duncan move quickly through space, with a sense of gratification. These distinctive movements are essential ingredients of their personalities.

Within the general framework of movement are smaller motions which characterize personality. Laban's "shadow movements" are dissipating gestures which have no expressive value at all. They can be efforts by the body to disguise fear or insecurity; Laban associates them with an attempt to mask egoism. These dissipating gestures are often automatic releases for misdirected energy. Diane Keaton in some of her early movie roles monumentalized "shadow" movements. As she developed as a film actor, she used less and less of these miniscule motions, particularly those which are centered in the face and hands. Often these movements are a result of an actor trying to force "spontaneity on camera." The labored effort produces an erratic energy.

By changing in any degree the physical aspects of personality, the film actor can communicate a different kind of person. If an actor is not interested in playing the "other," he can accept his physical personality, be at ease with whatever is projected by the camera when he is on screen. Relax and enjoy it.

5

THE FILM SCRIPT

A shooting script is a series of images, of shots, some of which pertain to action initiated by the character, some to reactions of the characters, some to objects which may or may not relate to the actor's immediate action, some to landscapes. Reading a shooting script requires that the actor understand in visual terms how the bits and pieces will come together in a final totality of story and character.

During his first reading of the script, the actor should note any inconsistencies that appear in character development. The script should delineate a believable character; the scenes should develop an unfolding of the layers of personality. Lines for the character should have meaning in terms of this unfolding of character; the actions should contribute to the refinement of character.

The potency of action in film far outweighs the power of words. While the character's actions should at times coincide with his verbal intentions, they should also occasionally serve as a counterpoint to his words if the character is to sustain interest. This kind of counterpoint action may not be obvious in a script; it may depend upon the way a director and actor choose to play either the action or the words. The actor should look for the subtle contradictions in the character, to add color to the role. If none are apparent in the script, the actor should make this a primary item of discussion in his meeting on the script with the director.

Discussing Script with Director

Most directors look forward to these script discussions with actors. Because the day-to-day business of shooting is so fraught with solving logistical difficulties, the director realizes there will be

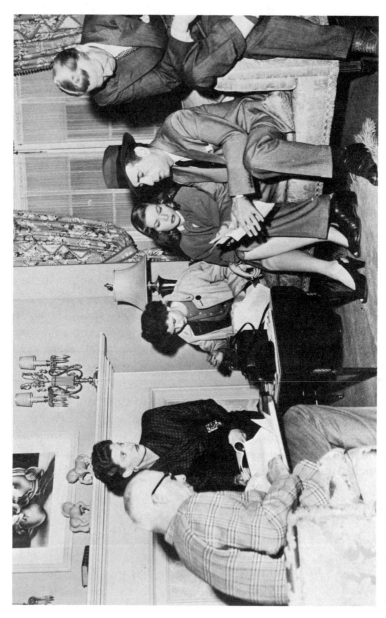

Lauren Bacall, Humphrey Bogart, and other cast members gather with director Howard Hawks (l.) for a script conference during The Big Sleep.

very little time during shooting for character changes. These early script meetings comprise the chief opportunities he and the actor have to make important changes in the character. Nothing should be held back at these meetings; at this stage, before the hectic activity of shooting begins, much can be accomplished to accommodate an actor's intuitive response to the character. Writers can be asked to rethink and rewrite scenes in terms of the actor's recommendations. At this stage the actor can be a major collaborator with the director and writer in forming the characterization. The careful reading and character analysis of a script is one of the actor's most important pre-production responsibilities.

On many occasions the actor will not receive the script very much in advance of the shooting date. Sometimes he is only given a copy of the scene in which he appears. The actor knows little more than the lines he will say. Unless the director has given him some information, he doesn't know if the scene is satiric, straightforward, or comic. Any permanent judgments about the quality or mood of the scene are inappropriate. After an initial discussion and mutual agreement with the director on the nature of the character, the experienced actor will learn his lines, and remain open during shooting to the suggested intentions of the director.

The film actor needs to be able to absorb quickly any line changes. Very often during rehearsals and shootings the director will find other qualities or actions in the scene springing from the actors' organic responses and he will make changes in lines on the spot. The scene itself may contain anywhere from three to twenty lines of dialogue, simple movements, or a complicated series of movements involving extras, animals, automobiles, and other mechanical assistance. In the best of situations the director has discussed with the actors the relationships, conflicts, and the cinematic values in the script. As often as not, the director and actor have met only for general discussions of the role.

Conveying the Meaning of the Script

The conditions that the actual shooting days engender make it essential that the actor do his homework on the script well in advance of shooting. In reading the shooting script and visualizing the events and characters in motion, the actor must develop a second sense about the weight and significance of specific actions and events as moving images on a screen. A script is a blueprint for the final product. It contains only the words and descriptions of actions. As he reads, the actor must imagine the action as a moving picture. Only in this way will the script convey its potency as a film.

Comprehension of the images as physical objects or action is a result of visual perception. However, the intellect and imagination almost immediately connect these images with ideas or emotions. We imbue the image/object/movement with meaning. These meanings change with the accumulation of images. The first impressions of character may be deepened or entirely changed as the progression of images continues. The associated meanings that the spectator attaches to the image will modify and refine the character as a film progresses. As he reads the script, the actor should note, then, the associations of meanings he himself makes in relation to the character, to the context of the settings in which the character is seen, and to the character's physical, mental, or emotional actions. As the actor reads, he forms a blueprint of character supported by imaginative associations.

The actor's initial, often intuitive, responses to character and action in the process of reading the script are extremely valuable. The actor acts as a clean slate upon which his initial impressions can write an organic evaluation of character. These initial impressions create inroads to the more complex elements of character and action. These intuitive responses will provide a central core for the characterization, one that acts as a touchstone for the actor during the technical distractions of shooting.

These first impressions of a character include both external traits, such as how the character walks, dresses, styles the hair, handles props, smiles, talks, or relaxes, and internal traits, such as the ways the character approaches new acquaintances or old friends, how he handles stress, or copes with problems. Internal traits may include the degree of self-esteem, or self-negation, and the level of optimism or pessimism in the character's orientation to life. It would benefit the actor to relate these traits to as many real people as he can. Making character judgments specific by relating them to real experience helps to recall these first impressions at will over a long period of time.

The script may also provoke questions regarding the character or the action. The logic of the progression of action or character may seem faulty. Director and actor should discuss why the character does what he does, whether the character changes, why he does, and which scenes focus on the change.

The mood and atmosphere of each scene should be discussed with the director in an informal manner. In these conferences with the director, the actor should share all of his impressions and thoughts regarding the script and the character.

The film characterization is one that relies on a melding of actor and character. If the actor can relate himself and his experiences directly to the character through line changes or actions that are true to both actor and character, he will create a subtle, organic characterization.

Understanding a film script demands both an imaginative, empathetic response and an intellectual analysis. Each method of comprehension is equally important. The preliminary intellectual analysis of the script will differentiate between supportive and dynamic dialogue and business, and will determine the emphasis in the characterization based on the amount of screen time which is given to any one or more particular objectives. The purpose of the intellectual analysis is to develop an overall concept of the role. Unless the actor knows the total effect of the character he plays, he is unlikely to be able to analyze the moment-by-moment rhythms of the character's actions. Not only does the actor have the script at his disposal for analysis, he also has the intellectual and intuitive knowledge of both the director and the screenwriter. The actor should learn what they have discovered in the character, what qualities they hope will be projected to the audience, and how they intend to focus on and underline the facets of character.

Examining the script for the inner meaning of the lines aids the actor in understanding the nature of the character. Very often what is meant by the character is something more or something less than what is said. The words of the character may be used to contradict his objectives, to over- or under-expose his meaning, or to cover up his intentions. The kinetic experience of reading the words, saying the words, allowing their basic qualities of rhythm and style to affect him, solidifies the inner meaning in the actor's consciousness and unconsciousness. When he moves to the shooting set, he no longer has to think or analyze what the character is doing, but simply does the action.

Since the film actor's performance consists of edited pieces of celluloid, and since the film actor works on his scenes out of sequence, thereby losing the opportunity to build up through momentum and rhythm of performance his character and conflict, he must find other ways of sustaining characterization out of sequence. One of Stanislavsky's methods that can help him with this task is the recreation and improvisation of situations outside the events of the script itself. This method of improvising situations outside the script gives the actor a firmer grasp on who the character is, and how he reacts towards the other characters, by placing him among them in any number of situations, some provoking conflict, others exploring environment and relationships. The actor then moves more easily and confidently into whatever sequence the shooting script calls for. The film actor must think of the character's life *happening* as the film is shot. In rehearsal or in the actor's solo work on himself he can improvise analogous situations to those in the script—so that even though he may shoot certain sections of that particular scene over a month's time, he has had the experience of going through the event, or a similar one, and can retain and recall the impetus for action more readily.

In his conferences with the director, the actor should also determine what his relationship to the camera will be, for it can influence and shape his performance. Some directors, such as Ingmar Bergman, always make certain the actor understands his relationship to the camera. What moments of the script are being reserved for the close-ups, what the director wants projected during the close-up, and how long individual close-ups will be held are all important questions for the actor to have answered. These will determine what gesture or detail the actor can select to convey those elements of characterization already determined in conferences to be essential.

Shots which call for silent reaction are as important as those shots which call for the action to initiate action in word or deed. Reaction is an aspect of acting that has been made an art in itself by

Jon Voight, John Boorman, Ronny Cox, and Burt Reynolds discuss the script during a break in the location shooting of Deliverance.

filmmakers. The art of listening, of assimilating new information, and responding primarily with the eyes is perhaps the most important adjustment for the stage actor to make to film acting. It demands that the actor be able to express thoughts naturally and to hold that expression using only his face. We must be able to see what the actor is thinking. Study of the script should include analysis and understanding of the variations in the character's silent reactions to others and to environments.

The nature of editing depends on the choice of the most interesting dramatic moments, and in many cases, a character's reaction is more dramatic than the words he says. The use of this silent image of expression is the most dynamic method film has to gather the spectator's attention. It is the basis of the special relationship between the spectator and the film because it is in these silent moments that the viewer creates his own words for what he sees. These silent moments will require the most subtlety and nuance in the actor's work. How to play these moments may well be left to the subconscious after some general discussion with the director. One thing is certain: the film actor cannot plan out what to do during these moments. He may have an idea of what the character is thinking or feeling, but he will not be able to plan how to express what he is feeling or thinking. That is best left to the moments of shooting when the actor can give his total concentration to the character's action, and allow his face to register whatever is provoked by the action. Allowing something to occur is dependent upon the actor putting up no barriers to the action. The greatest acting flaw in silent moments is overplaying or structuring a reaction.

As vitally important to characterization as script understanding and analysis is, it should be augmented by a technical knowledge of how the script will be transferred to the shooting schedule. The high cost of making a film prevents producers and directors from shooting the script totally in sequence. To facilitate the shooting, the script is divided into categories having similar requirements.

The film script is usually first broken down into two general categories: studio shots and out-of-studio shots. These initial groupings allow the director to shoot scenes with similar requirements at one time.

The studio shots are grouped according to the separate settings each requires. The out-of-studio shots are divided into exterior shots and interior shots. Each general category of shot is then grouped according to the special conditions needed for each shot. For example, the time of day, the cast members needed for any shot sequence, the weather conditions, the use of synchronous sound recorded along with the picture, may each be common factors in any particular grouping of shots. Although these divisions facilitate the shooting, they mean that the action necessarily will be shot out of sequence.

Although every shot in the script is numbered in sequence, it is almost impossible for the actor during the shooting to keep track of each shot's place in the script progression. He must depend on the director to inform him where and how each shot fits into the script. As each shot is made, it is labelled with the pertinent information. If a shot is filmed repeatedly, it is given a "take" number. There may, then, be several takes of the same shot. At some point when he is satisfied with the shot, the director will designate a certain take for printing. These "print" takes comprise the "dailies" or the "rushes." Whether or not the actor chooses to look at the daily is a matter of individual choice. It may help him keep track of his performance, or it may make him overly self-conscious about his work.

The actor should bear in mind that a director may decide to combine elements from many different takes to make the final print—a gesture from take two, a line from take six, a crossing movement from take three, and so on. This is part of the editing process which will produce the final version of the print. Actors watching the final edited print may have no memory of having performed the role in that specific way during one or two shots.

Special Demands of the Medium

Whether the location be on a sound stage or in an outdoor location, the actor is surrounded by a mass of equipment and a crowd of technicians who operate the equipment. With the cameras are the director and his various assistants, the producers or their representatives, still photographers and publicity people. In the background may be a group of people touring the set. The director

A studio set for Lydia creates not only location but can recreate wind or snowstorm.

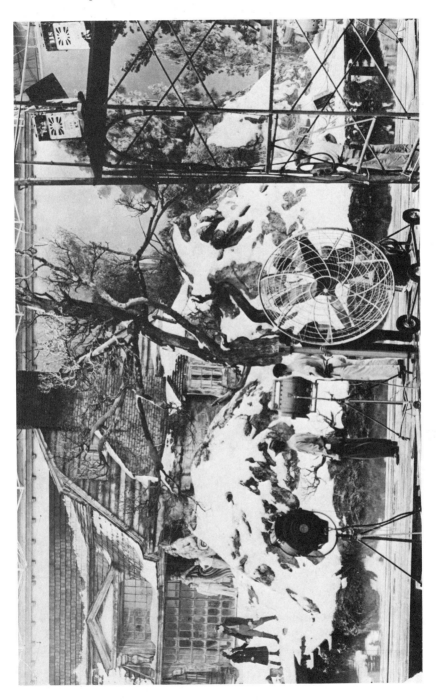

will run through the scene quickly, making last-minute changes in lines or movements. The cameraman will hold a brief conference with the director plotting out the mechanics of shooting, and setting up for any angles to be included in the takes ahead. If the actor has a stand-in, he himself may sit back, using this time to prepare for the scene. When the cameras are ready, the director may run through the scene two or three times more before turning on the cameras. Inevitably, during the shooting something will go wrong. A vase or chair will accidentally be knocked over, an actor will say the wrong line, the director will get his feet tangled in the cables and fall, the fog machine will quit, a camera will break down, an actor will shift out of the right light, and the director will "cut" the camera. After the problems are solved, the next take begins. The actors will repeat the take until the director is satisfied he has what he wants, and designates the take a print. Directors can totally change the movement given to an actor during a take—either from the purely physical (crossing to there instead of here), to entering or moving on a different line, or dropping a line entirely, leaving the actor only the movement. It may take an hour to shoot what will be fifteen seconds of screen time.

These conditions can produce extraordinary tension within the actor as he tries to remember his words, his movements, the director's instructions, the chalk marks, the microphones, and tries to look as though he's not under a bank of hot, blinding lights. When he's succeeded for one take, he then must spend an enormous amount of time waiting for the next one, while the director visualizes the angles, makes scene changes, or the technicians move equipment. Then for the close-up shots the actor must recreate the rhythms, the intentions, and the motivations of these prior scenes. With a camera two or three feet from him, a director sitting not one foot away from him (for he can sit anywhere so long as he is not in range of the camera), the actor must react to the conditions of the scene. To add to the complication, the character the actor is reacting to may be played by an actor who has already left the set to go to lunch. In the midst of a serious scene in which a great amount of conflict or passion is being generated, the actor must seem unaware both of the director's critical eye so close upon him, and of the camera whirring away behind or to one side or above him.

In the midst of this mechanical intrusion upon his concentration the film actor performs, and waits. At times film acting seems to be 90 percent waiting. Long periods of waiting tend to deaden the actor's sensitivity to the action, to lull him into lethargy. Then, when called, he must shake off the lethargy and inertia and rise to play the role. During his performance he does not have the response of the theatre audience—the organism that sends messages to the actor with its laughter or silences. Film technicians must necessarily be concentrating on details other than the actor's performance, such as the correct placement of the lights, the changing of focus during the scene, and the movement of the camera. The film actor has very little feedback from this audience when his performance is going well. His confidence must be placed in the director, and in his own knowledge and intuition about his work. Once confident, the film actor must give himself over to the sense of immediacy and improvisation needed for the scene.

The insects in *The Hellstrom Chronicle*, a narrated documentary shot in micro-photography, offer clues to the techniques which will overcome whatever limitations the elements of space, time, and edited images place on acting for the camera. The insects were powerful "actors," as were the mechanical models of King Kong and the great white shark in *Jaws*, because they did not intrude upon the camera's eye. The insects followed at their own speed a set of programmed instincts, a series of seemingly trivial and pedestrian actions, while the camera focused in on them in close-ups, allowing the audience to invest the action with meaning. The face of an insect in close-up is as interesting in raw and menacing detail as that of any movie villain. What is distinct about the insects and mechanical monsters is that they give no indication that they care about being watched by the camera, or that they are concerned about anything other than the immediate accomplishment of their objectives. So the film actor must think and analyze *before* shooting the meaning and intention of the character and the script, the effect of angles upon interpretation of the scene, and the power of editing to create character. These elements must be absorbed and hidden in his technique so that they appear only as a set of instincts rather than skills or knowledge.

He must learn to use the advantages in realistic playing that film acting offers. For example, while the stage actor must treat an artificially produced prop as though it were real, the film actor has the real thing in his hands and can respond naturally to it. There is no pretending involved, no cheating allowed. The film actor does not have to convince the audience that the prop he uses is the real thing, as is the case very often with the stage actor who is using a cardboard prop. The same holds true for the effect of using real locations.

Relating to a real environment is much easier than having to convince the audience that a painted set is a cabin in the Rockies, or a hut in Tahiti. If an actor is filmed in a real snowstorm, there is no acting involved in his being cold or chilled. He will be chilled by the real thing. Anthony Mann especially likes filming westerns for this reason because "the elements make them much greater as actors than if they were in a room. Because they have to shout above the winds, they have to suffer, they have to climb mountains." As naturally as the insects, these actors Mann refers to are organically responding to their natural environments. There is no way anyone can plan a reaction to a real dust storm or to the crossing of a real river or desert. The real props and the real environments evoke in the actor his individual physical responses unadorned by artifice.

It is important that the film actor recognize the special conditions of making a film, conditions that will affect his shaping and preserving of the image of character he has chosen for the film. He must consider the effect of montage upon the delineation of the character. As the spectator sees the character unfolding, he may glean information from not only the words and facial gestures used by the actor, but also through the director's intercutting of other images, such as a hand gesture, or the reaction of another face. More than other actors, the film actor must be aware of the psychological effect of editing techniques that will influence the audience and make his moves either more powerful or less, depending upon the dissipation of the actor's energy. Ideally, he will be able to retain an impression of what a shot of a clenched hand or a distant, unruly crowd might add to his image, or be made aware of these editing techniques by the director. Montage or the rhythmic composition of film shots will alter the image of character, and if the actor is not to be at odds with the image that is developed through editing techniques, he must be aware of their effect. In an

The addition of sensory detail such as saturation in water adds to the sensual quality of this scene from The Night of the Iguana *with Ava Gardner.*

ideal situation, the actor would have the benefit of knowing what editing would be done on the film. Most film actors, however, are not allowed to participate in the editing of the film, and so are dependent upon the director's best use of the footage available.

Having absorbed the mechanical environment of filmmaking, the technical intrusion of the camera, and the knowledge that what he chooses as images of character depend upon his time and space relationship to the camera, the film actor must release his creative powers from that technical knowledge and, in a childlike state, respond to the event and conflict. His safest harbor is a trusting and open relationship with the film director, who may then collaborate with the actor, rather than use his physical presence and personality, to produce character.

This is the work of the film actor: to seem to be where the camera will reveal him to be, rather than surrounded by machinery; to choose gestures which suit his focal distance from the camera; and to separate his planned elements of performance from his on-camera playing, making it all seem like improvisation. His major collaborator, if he is allowed one at all, is the film director.

6

THE DIRECTOR

You must never let the actor know when you're going to give him the custard in the choppers. . . . The wisest technique is to con your victim into a sense of security and then slip it to him.
— Del Lord, comedy director for Mack Sennett

Even when directing an actor who would get a pie in the face, many directors feel the need to keep the actor ignorant about what is going to happen, preferring to capture a spontaneous reaction. Today the custard is different, and directors don't always give it to the actor in the "choppers," but the conning of the "victim" is still happening . . . and often with very rewarding results.

It is true that an actor need not necessarily understand everything he is doing. Very often an intellectual understanding may make an actor too self-conscious about the form of his work. Certainly, if the actor tries to achieve an intellectual understanding of a particular line or scene while in the midst of shooting, he may set up obstacles for himself. He may lose the spontaneity of the scene's action. An actor must not direct himself while in the act of acting. An intellectual understanding, though, is helpful before shooting to start the actor's creative juices flowing in thinking about the character. Such understanding is the support for the work of the imagination. If a poet wants to write an ode to deep-sea fishing, he must first know something about that activity. The facts are important. So with acting the actor/poet must know the facts about the character and the narrative of the film script in order to begin his creative interpretation.

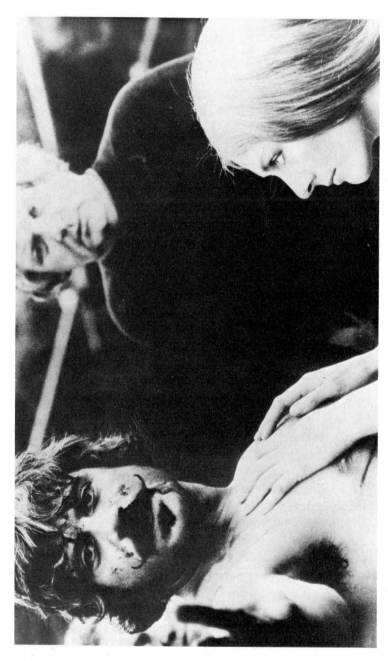

Ken Russell watches a scene from The Devils *with Oliver Reed and Vanessa Redgrave.*

There has always been a special relationship between the director and the actor. Much discussion has been centered around the question of whether the actor is a pawn in the director's vision of the chess game. There are actors' directors, who do all they can to awaken the actor's imagination and refine his abilities, and there are action directors, who would as soon talk to a horse as to an actor. Certainly, much of the decision-making regarding character development is left to the director. It is generally his view of the characters that is followed in the initial interpretation, and shaped in the editing room. Footage of any actor can be manipulated to create the impression the director has in mind for the character and the scene. Almost all male directors have made incarnate their visions of the ideal woman, and kept those visions alive by casting similar types in each movie: Hitchcock's cold, unreachable blonde, Griffith's pure virgin-child, Arthur Penn's independent thinker.

Some directors handle actors with a sense of violence before an emotionally charged scene. Some belittle the actor's desires to question the script's and character's meaning. Some physically manipulate the actor to put him in the desired attitude. In *Way Down East*, Griffith placed Lillian Gish on a moving ice floe which began to split dangerously, and automatically captured the corresponding physical reactions. There was no need for Miss Gish to "act" afraid. Her body was put in jeopardy, and its mechanisms of terror and self-preservation asserted themselves naturally.

In *The Music Lovers*, Ken Russell placed Glenda Jackson and Richard Chamberlain in a cramped coach compartment, turned the music up to a loud volume, rocked the coach, and had the actors repeat the scene over and over until he had the emotional level he envisioned for the scene. According to Russell, Glenda Jackson noted and made use of the new dimensions and meanings these physical circumstances brought to the scene. The psychophysical technique of directing used a physical means to evoke the psychological action of the scene.

Antonioni has said of directing an actor, "I had to direct her almost with a sense of violence. Before every scene, I had to put her in a state of mind appropriate to that particular scene. If it was a sad scene, I had to make her cry; if it was a happy scene, I had to make her laugh." These directors have discovered that the physical circumstances on the set and during the shooting will affect,

Director Nicolas Roeg and Julie Christie during the making of Don't Look Now.

change, and guide an actor. Putting actors inside a rocking coach, and assaulting them with high-volume music, will produce certain high-level emotional states in them. If the director is wise in his choices, that state will be exactly what he needs in the scene. Some actors will use music or poetry in the moments before shooting to gear themselves up to the level of action and emotion required. It is a way of unlocking the inner resources of the actor, resources he may not be conscious of, and therefore, able to use at will. Directors such as Ingmar Bergman, Martin Scorcese, and Bernardo Bertolucci are said to be able to put the actor in the proper psychological circumstances before a scene so that all the unplanned, psychophysical gestures are released naturally by the actor—playing with eyeglasses, shaking one's head, looking down or away from the other person. In an interview in *Rolling Stone*, Marlon Brando refers to these kinds of gestures as "the essence of reality" revealing the low threshold of fear each person has of encounter with another.

Many directors, however, fear to give rein to the actor's automatic responses and call for a set reaction which allows only the most superficial of gestures. Each director is an individual striving to put his vision on film, and the actor who hasn't been able to discuss the interpretation with the director is at the mercy of the director or the writer during the shooting. The director will have his ideas about the character, the writer will have his notions, the actor may have a third interpretation. Some directors will want to discuss every single detail of the character; some will want only to be involved with the composition of the film; and others, as Marlon Brando says in the same *Rolling Stone* interview, "wait for you to bring everything to them." Lucky is the actor who has a director waiting for his "everything" and ready to give him any help he needs during the strenuous emotional scenes.

Although Pudovkin advised that the actor try to "create and preserve a feeling of the sum total of the separate fragments of acting as a single image, enlivened by himself," it remains one of the most difficult tasks for today's actor, limited as he is by the director's attitude toward him, by the secrecy in which many directors keep their intentions of the character's effect, and by the actor's own lack of understanding of the effect of each shot and angle. Directors such as Antonioni and Polanski want the actors to

Director Peter Glenville becomes actively involved in the emotional content of the scene in Summer and Smoke.

remain will-less automatons, untouched by any influence outside the director's. It is therefore up to the actor to learn whom to trust with his vulnerability. With a director such as Antonioni, the only way to successful characterization for an actor may be to convince himself to remain open to the moment, to allow himself to be concerned only with reacting to this particular experience as the director has described it. The person of the actor is very much involved with the character in film, and the actor should not "get in the way of himself" through arbitrarily selected gestures, vocal intonations, or interpretations of character. There are many directors who can detect qualities of personality and idiosyncrasies of behavior which are outside the actor's own consciousness, and bring these out by carefully selected exercises.

Pudovkin, using a young self-conscious non-actor, wanted a certain "sweet, shy smile" from him. He made the young man bend over and hold his feet for a length of time before giving him the signal to straighten up. He told the young boy only that he would feel good when he could straighten up (as indeed any of us would inevitably feel after holding that awkward posture). After a time, he told the boy to straighten up, and as he was doing so, Pudovkin interrupted the movement with a question. The young boy, being inexperienced, reacted to him in exactly the way Pudovkin anticipated, with a smile broken through with an undertone of shy confusion. This result depends upon an inventive director who can sense what the natural reaction of the actor or person is going to be.

Should an experienced actor withhold himself from being manipulated in this way? It would seem inadvisable to do so, if by consenting, and freeing oneself to the moment, fresh and unplanned responses might surface. These methods are ways of stimulating an actor to respond in a different manner, just as actors' methods often use paintings or images to explore character response. Most actors try to find new means of tricking their technical knowledge and techniques—surprising themselves in the hopes of connecting with an intuitive response. Italian director Federico Fellini spends hours with his actors at meals and in conversations outside shooting in order to find these kinds of natural, psychophysical gestures and responses which are not restrained or overcultivated by the person. Once Fellini finds such responses, he looks for places to use them in his films, believing

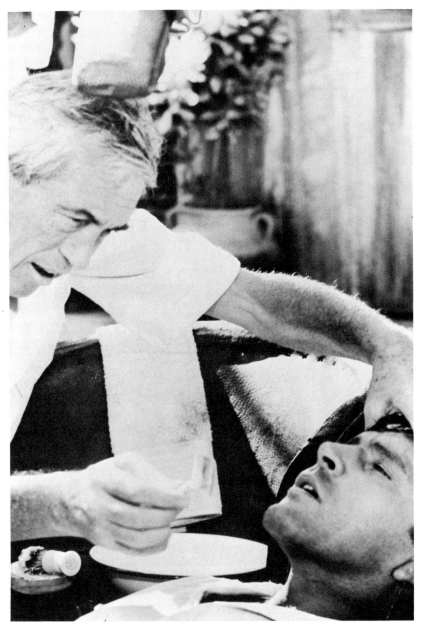

Director John Huston works out the logistics of the shaving scene between Ava Gardner and Richard Burton in The Night of the Iguana.

"that each actor is a human reality and therefore different. Each has a certain experience. I try to tap that."

Both Godard and Antonioni have kept the cameras on and used the footage of actors not acting, but being themselves. Godard, for example, left in footage of Anna Karina correcting herself in the middle of delivering a line in *A Woman Is a Woman* to point up the duality of her character: insecurity beneath an aggressive exterior. Robert Altman lets the cameras shoot when the actors are unaware, and uses some of the spontaneous reactions that occur. There are often occasions in the theatre when an actor wishes to recapture the spontaneity of a reaction evoked during a rehearsal improvisation. They are often difficult to recreate, changed as they are by the actor's consciousness of them. In film it is possible to record these the instant they happen, ready then for use in the final print.

There are as many directorial techniques for eliciting spontaneous reactions as there are organic responses. Some directors may reshoot a take twenty to thirty times looking for the kind of frustrated fatigue that such an experience automatically produces. Others, realizing the potency of the camera to provoke the spectator in the cinema into acting himself, find ways of getting the actor to do nothing, which can then be "read" by the viewer as a spontaneous reaction which seems natural to the situation. In effect, the viewer places meaning and substance into the neutral face. Rouben Mamoulian instructed Garbo to think of nothing for the last shot in *Queen Christina*, and like an Oriental theatre mask, her face allows the spectator to fill in the meaning from his own experiences.

Through external devices, directors have often manipulated actors into following the logically rhythmic progression of an action. Vincente Minnelli, giving a direction to George Hamilton, told him to cross to a table, count five, pick up a pencil, and say the line. To a method-trained actor in that same scene, Minnelli gave no specific directions, but discussed the motivations and intentions of the action. Film critic John Kobal has recounted the story of Josef Von Sternberg's telling Marlene Dietrich to "Count six, and look at the lamp post as if you couldn't live without it." In these ways actors who do too much, not enough, or arhythmically execute action can give the effect of a direct action unimpeded by dissipating gestures, an effect that will serve the needs of the story, the character, and perhaps, most importantly, the rhythmic composition of the film.

The great Russian director Sergei Eisenstein based his methods of film direction on principles that had been worked out by Stanislavsky and the Moscow Art Theatre, and these methods serve as a basis today for all creative work in film. For Eisenstein, a major tool in directing actors was to guide them to use their own personal emotional experiences as a basis for the unfolding of emotion in the character. Eisenstein encouraged the actor to "arouse in his imagination a series of concrete pictures or situations appropriate to the theme," observing them like a film running through the actor's mind. The key word in this statement is not "imagination" but "concrete." To evoke the proper feelings, ones which are not stereotyped, the actor cannot play the major emotions such as love and hate, but must select for scanning in his mind's eye the concrete physical details which surround these emotions. Eisenstein recounts an inner monologue in the imaginative recreation of a character contemplating suicide after he has embezzled a sum of money. Each detail of the inner monologue is a description of a physical detail—"the eye of a neighbor fixed upon him," "the whisper of censure and the murmur of voices." The emotions are housed within the physical responses. This inner monologue is similar to a shooting script in that all Eisenstein's images are visual, physical, and like film itself, each image has its own angle and distance. On imagining his return from prison, Eisenstein's inner monologue or interior film would conjure up the "floor of the hall . . . newly varnished and . . . a new mat outside my door. From below . . . the old janitor . . . stares up the stairwell." Out of this imagistic detail the proper emotions will be called to life for the actor's use in the scene. From this point the actor can let them develop into other feelings and gestures in response to the situation or the other characters. This kind of approach was for Eisenstein the first stage of the actor's work, the second being a "compositional elaboration of these elements" of behavior, which requires the elimination of every action that is accidental or dissipating, and the refinement of these elements to the highest level of expressiveness, one that is pure, clear, and communicative.

In creating these mental pictures of concrete, physical details corresponding to the demands of the theme or character, the actor guards against a fixed characterization by forcing himself to respond to the situation in the moment rather than preplanning a response which can too easily become mechanical. The physical details surrounding the scene can be changed to include other persons, other rooms—either more or less threatening—which can help to prevent the actor from using one response, no matter how well it suited the situation. Many directors help the actor to explore the situation by asking him to respond a different way each time the scene is shot. By consciously trying new reactions or objectives, the actor does not fall into the pitfall of learning to love his own imagination's work, hanging on to a particularly good response until it becomes stale.

A director most actors have enjoyed working with is Elia Kazan, who has prompted actors to give their finest performances by allowing them rehearsal time to develop character details, to show him all that they have, and in discussion to choose the best suited to both the directorial vision and the actor's concept. Kazan works the actors, trying new ideas. His sensitive perception of the acting mechanism gives the actor confidence in himself to create.

The actor's best insurance is to build a rapport with the director which is open and trusting. Without the security of knowing that the director will tell him when he is going too far or not far enough, the actor can become fearful and defensive. In order to protect himself, then, he may resort to standardized gestures from previous films, and cut himself off from any experimentation of behavior. The role of the director is often that of a guardian of the actor's self-consciousness or a parental surrogate monitoring action with approval or disapproval. Many directors do not mind playing such roles, agreeing with Joseph Losey that, "When you have a good actor who knows what you want and is continually looking for things inside of himself, and knows that you are not going to make a fool of him either on the set or on the screen, then you can see extraordinary things happen."

Such care and guidance offsets the risk the film actor takes in turning over his performance to the many controls inherent in the filmmaking process. Both director and actor must strive to create an environment in which playing before the camera is forgotten. In order to meet the demands of every actor's insecurities and needs, the film director works to influence the actor in a person-to-person relationship, using rehearsals and improvisations to discover how close to the character the actor is, and to use the actor's own instincts, intuition, and body language as an expression of character. For directors, casting is the most important element in film because the essence of personality is revealed so dynamically by the camera. The closer the actor is to the manner, physical appearance, and personality of the character, the more time there is that can be spent on developing the particular images of character. The actor, too, can then trust in his own personality mechanisms, feeling confident that the director has seen qualities which do not have to be manufactured. The ideal casting, according to John Huston, is "when the personality lends itself exquisitely to the part and when that personality has the added attribute of being technically a fine actor so he can control his performance."

II
Close-Up Views

7

MECHANICS OF
FILM ACTING

Every art has its own specifications of materials and environment: the painter his canvas and colors; the sculptor his clay, stone, chisel, and iron; and the dancer his body and the rhythms of music or sound. Each has a space in which the work is executed. Acting began in a relatively small space as a cathartic ritual—the reenactment of the day's hunt by tribal members gathered around the evening's fire. Over the years the theatre's acting space has evolved and changed from a simple platform to massive, ornate auditoriums to the rigidly confined and enclosed spaces used by Jerzy Grotowski in his work with the Polish Lab Theatre.

Filmmaking combines both a rigidly marked space for the actor and an outer environment which can be a constructed set, an outdoor environmental location, or "found" buildings, streets, and towns which are taken over by the filming crew for the making of the movie.

The mechanical operations involved in filmmaking require the actor to adjust any external theatrical techniques to a new set of techniques defined by the camera and its specifications of operation. Examining the differences between the materials and environment of theatre and film acting will illustrate which theatrical techniques can be adapted, restrained, or entirely eliminated by the film actor.

Three major differences between the two media are found in the elements of space, time, and image. In film acting, the actor has two arenas of physical space: the immediate circle around him which is marked by the camera's lens, and an outer circle of environment in which he may be photographed as part of the locale and background. The actor must perform within these two arenas, occasionally without knowing which one the director is shooting him in.

Within these two general circles of environment are other areas of restrictions. On a soundstage set, marks are indicated for the actors' movements. In making a cross from one direction to another on the set, the film actor must stop at or "hit" a certain mark in order to remain within camera range and focus. For stylized groupings, such as a shot of three profiles, actors must remain still and in close proximity to each other. The focus may also change on cue within this kind of specialized group shot; so there may be additional restrictions on the actors' use of dialogue within the time frame of the shot. The actors may, for example, have to put pauses in their speeches to allow time for the camera to make movement changes or focus changes.

In order to retain the composition the director has selected for the shot, the actors must not only hit their marks, but also remain on mark for the designated duration of the shot. Film is a rectangular frame of changing images. Paintings and photographs freeze the figures in a certain composition. In film the actor must be able to hold his position and sustain his concentration for certain amounts of time determined by the director.

The tight circle of concentration which defines the close-up focuses the actor's attention on the areas of thought and feeling, response and reaction. In the larger circle of environment the actor must seem at ease, relating organically to a manufactured or natural environment of place and time.

Time in film is reduced to the length of the shot—the number of seconds during which the camera is running. This determines and limits what the actor can do while the machine observes and records him. A long close-up obviously makes the actor's work easier since he then has the time to move into and out of a thought or feeling. Since the actor's work is to provide material for the quilt of piecemeal expressions patched together from longer images for directorial effects, he hopes for a large segment of camera time in which to develop the progression of his reaction and responses, thus affecting the consistency of the image. Many actors today are using a technique of pausing before they begin a line, using the pause to look toward another character or execute some physical gesture. The actor's efforts must include enough material from his inner resources to create not only logical images of emotion, but also images which will have a continuum of relationship to each other, no matter how they are edited later. This continuum of response is only accessible to the actor who develops an understanding of the whole character, the effect of environment and conflict upon character, and the capacity of the camera to heighten the impact of physical gesture.

Actors new to film work quickly develop hindsight with the experience of doing end sequences first. Weeks later, knowing the character so much better, they often feel they would have done something different during those first days of shooting. This hindsight is valuable knowledge; it promotes a more thoughtful approach to character in the following film. The actor will read the next script with more care, responding to the character in terms of the mechanics of making the film. He will consider what is important to retain in a non-sequential shooting schedule. Over several experiences in film acting, the actor will quickly develop foresight, intuitively isolating what character elements are important to bear in mind as the shooting begins and progresses.

SPACE, TIME, AND EDITED IMAGES

The actor's body itself is space filled with bone, muscle, and impulse, with liquid that is flowing in an ebb and tide of release and constraint within the space and relationships outlined in the script. The camera, a mechanical object which can bore into and reveal what is under the surface of any expression, is a partner in the enterprise. The film actor must become aware of the depth and breadth of his relationship with the camera. Does it register the nuances of his expressions or does it exaggerate and overemphasize what the actor believes are his naturalistic gestures? What effect does the working environment have upon the actor's ability to develop a relationship with the camera, the script, and other characters? The bank of cameras, the heat of the lights, the space between the actor and the camera—all these elements influence the actor's work, setting up limitations and possible barriers to it, until the actor becomes accustomed to the working conditions and operates within them as readily as any machine or prop. Only then can he concentrate his dynamic energy of creating character into the time, setting, and event of the script.

Work on a film has its own set of programmed actions which are laid out according to what the camera can do, and what the director and editor will do later with the filmed sequences. When an actor appears on the stage, he has two or three hours to develop character. He uses the emotional momentum of his first act to refine and provoke his actions in the next acts. Offstage, there is relative quiet surrounding the triangle of the play, the actors, and the audience. As he moves through the action of the play, the audience's focus and interest expressed through laughter or held silences prompts him to alter his performance slightly in response. Through the actor's self-exposure in the role, he can precipitate a similar vulnerability in the spectator to the character or narrative.

In film an actor appears to us on a piece of celluloid projected on a screen. He himself is probably at work on the next film, or at home reading other scripts, and cannot respond or alter his performance based on our reactions. The actor's work has been completed months before on a set or soundstage, surrounded then by machines and technicians who may have been observing his work for the effects of the lighting on his hair, rather than monitoring the truth of his action and behavior in the scene. The actor may have spent four hours at a makeup table and another two waiting for the shots to be set up. He must play his scene within certain marks determined by the focal distances used by the cameraman. Pojecting his voice is unnecessary since the microphone will pick up whatever volume he uses, and technicians can change it. He will shoot a variety of short scenes lasting anywhere from one to nine minutes. A day's work may cover three minutes of completed screen time. The scenes in the day's work may not be in consecutive relationship to the one before or the one after.

Instead of entering onto a theatre box or circle and recreating for three hours the life of a character, the screen actor enters into a smaller acting space (though he may be surrounded by the Rocky Mountains), and in this smaller box he has to slice his theatre

A television studio—ATV—at Elstree.

performance into three or four moments of time. He hopes to be able to match his creativity in one day's shooting with the next, to produce a whole entity imbued with logic and imagination.

The discontinuity in shooting scenes is for many actors the most difficult task in film acting. Location and setups may require shooting the love scene the first day on the set with another actor met only fifteen minutes earlier, and then shooting the first meeting between the lovers two weeks later (by which time the actors may have grown to hate one another). It demands concentration, imagination, and the ability to recreate instantly the attitude the character has going into the scene. Each actor has to find his own solution to this problem. The exceptional actor Paul Muni described it as the actor's need to "make the additional effort of mentally coordinating his lines before the camera. He must be ready to reorient to the state of the scene preceding the one now being shot, and absorb its effect so that his work will show the proper emotional development." Absorbing the effect of a previous scene is not an intellectual task, but a physical and emotional one. Not only must the level of emotional intensity be reached, but the body must also reflect this level of involvement. This is especially difficult if the character moves from an interior location to an exterior. Interior scenes are shot at one time, exteriors at another; there may be weeks between shooting an exit from a building from the point of view of the character inside the building and filming his movement outside the building. The emotion may require a build-up from the time the character is inside the building to the last shot of him going down the street. The actor has to be sensitive to this kind of acting problem in films.

Some actors sit quietly gathering their kinetic forces, others walk continuously from place to place, rehearsing their lines. Others work crossword puzzles, play cards, or read. The script-continuity person will handle the technical responsibility of seeing that the actor's clothing, posture, and props match the previous scene; the unbroken thread of emotional response must be in the actor's mind and body, ready for recall at a moment's notice. Very often in watching movies we may notice a change in the actor from one cut to another. There may be a mismatch in the actor's level of intellectual interest or emotional intensity, just as there is often a slightly noticeable difference in hairstyle or makeup. This mis-

Note the concentration of Bogart in this Key Largo setup, in contrast to the relaxation of the camera crew and technicians.

match in attitude jars us; we are aware something is "off," wrong with the image. This points out the difficulty of the actor's work in matching the level of interest and intensity from shot to shot. The rite of passage from one scene's shooting to the next should include re-experiencing the natural flow of events which will enable the actor to pick up the same thread and unwind a bit more of it.

The Russian filmmaker Pudovkin suggested that the shooting script be rearranged into a new sequence for rehearsals "enabling nearer approximation of the shots in the actor's role, thus giving him larger pieces of united inner movement." This rehearsal script might include the substitution of equivalent actions for certain parts of the shooting script. The choice of equivalents is based on the type and degree of obstacle which the character must overcome in order to attain his objective. For example, in a rehearsal script Pudovkin substitutes a door which must be broken through for a river that must be crossed in the shooting script. Breaking through the door mobilizes the actor's emotional drive and kinetic energies to succeed in accomplishing his objective. He then transfers these responses to the situation and objectives in the shooting script. In this circumstance the actor is like an athlete preparing his body to respond by sparring or jogging in place. A detailed rehearsal period in which the actor can make these inner links between all the shots is helpful in sharpening the actor's ability to perform at a moment's notice again and again during the actual shooting.

During rehearsal time improvisations based on situations and circumstances involving the characters in the intervals between the written scenes aid the actor in grasping a fuller notion of the whole life of his character. These kinds of rehearsal techniques are the ideal, of course. In these times the high cost of shooting a film precludes this kind of work. However, the improvisational technique is being used in films. Such films as Robert Altman's *Nashville* are constructed out of improvisations and disclose a growing interest in the development of movies as an actor's art. Some directors shoot improvisations in order not to miss those moments of inspiration and organic responses which often occur spontaneously in rehearsals.

Unless the film actor realizes the effect upon characterization that shooting out of sequence can have, he may find it difficult to construct a clear, precise, and detailed absorption of the overall scope of the role. If the scene's emotional range metaphorically calls for the music of violins and the actor comes on as a brass band, there is no harmonic segue from one moment to the next. He must tune his own instrument if no rehearsals are allotted in the production schedule, and use any means of play or concentration device to make the inner connections between scenes.

An important distinction of film acting is related to the fact that the camera can move. In the theatre, we remain at a certain distance from the actor, rarely able to distinguish any subtle changes in his face. Our attention is focused on the stage actor through the use of changes in the compositional details of the stage picture. Characters onstage turn to look or listen to another, and the audience focuses on that actor. We are not aware of the patterns of facial expressions on each of the turning characters; the physical postures and bodily attitudes are signals to the audience to turn its attention elsewhere. In film, the camera's movement directs our focus with a vehemence. We cannot "not look" as in the theatre, where, if we wish, we can wander over the faces in a crowd scene or examine the set details while we listen to the voice of the main character.

In film, the actor's face can fill the screen, and only in film do we ever get such a close look at an actor's face. Since the camera enlarges every movement, the film actor must be much more economical in the use of gesture and physical postures. Those which are used should not convey any artifice. The film actor is given the opportunity to work with the small details of his face, allowing the camera to move in and catch the nuances of facial expressions. In film, as opposed to theatre, even actors in crowd scenes have the opportunity to reveal particular and individual responses which will be examined in close-up. In the theatre, a group of people turning to focus on the main character remains a group force, a mass of interesting compositional details.

In the theatre, the actor must be able to project his voice to carry the distance required by the size of the building. He should be able to modulate his voice so that even his whisper will carry the necessary emotion. In film, not only will microphones and sound regulators control the vocal elements, but also the sound editor can literally change the way an actor speaks. Many directors mention the need in film to remove the sound "clicks" that occur when an actor's mouth is dry from nervous tension. The actor's voice can be cut from certain sequences in the film, and the sequence will appear a silent action. A voice can be dubbed for any actor in film, if and when the need arises. Appearing before us in person, the theatre actor has much more responsibility for his own performance, and needs a great deal of physical stamina to carry him through the three hours of performance. Tremendous physical stamina is also required in film acting—to repeat actions that require varying amounts of physical exertion time after time after time.

The film character we see may actually be an amalgamation of many actors. An actor playing the part of a musical composer might, for instance, have his voice dubbed by someone proficient in doing foreign dialects. In scenes at the piano a skilled pianist's hands might be filmed instead of the actor's hands and an unknown but excellent vocalist's voice may be substituted for the actor's singing voice. An actress with a beautiful face but unshapely legs might still be cast if the legs of a dancer were used in any necessary leg close-ups. The nude body of the woman killed in the shower in *Psycho* was not the body of Janet Leigh. Marni Nixon may not be recognized by filmgoers in person, yet her voice is familiar as the singing voice of Eliza Doolittle as played by Audrey Hepburn in *My Fair Lady*. The voice of the Lone Ranger in the recent film *The Lone Ranger* was entirely dubbed by another actor. Mercedes McCambridge's voice was the voice of the possessed young girl in certain scenes that Linda Blair played in *The Exorcist*. This sort of substitution is standard in film. Only in film would we accept this synthetic manufacture of character, since only on film are we unaware of these substitutions when they are technically well executed.

This synthetic manufacture establishes the film actor as more an instrument for the director than is the theatre actor. When an actor walks onstage, his performance is totally in his hands. Much of the film actor's performance depends on the angle the director chooses to use in shooting him. The actor may be doing a remarkable job of recreating emotion, but if the scene is shot over his shoulder, we will see only what reflects itself in his back. What may seem to the actor a particularly prized moment of expression —the clue to his character—may be cut out by the editor or director for reasons known only to themselves. An actor may search for the right shoes to wear as a certain character, only to discover they will never be seen in any of the shots the director plans to take. Wearing the shoes may help the actor discover some aspect of the character, but the audience might never share that detail. An actor may work out a mode of walking which seems suited to the character; an editor can change the tempo and rhythm of that walk to some extent. It is the director's intentions and visions of character that are reflected in the final editing of the film.

8

INFLUENCE OF CINEMATIC ELEMENTS ON CHARACTER IMAGE

The communication of film characterization is greatly influenced by various cinematic techniques: the use of various angles, the actor's distance from the camera, character and scene lighting, the details included in the frame, and the camera's movement and its effect on the size of the image. The effects and limitations of camera techniques change the nature of the actor's work both as actor and as character.

CAMERA ANGLES AND SHOTS

There are as many variations of shooting angles as there are directors and cameramen to try them. Over-the-shoulder, full front, from above, from below, right profile, left profile, from the back, or on a diagonal are some of the basic angles, any of which can be accomplished by a stationary or moving camera.

Within the acting space the film actor must not be distracted by the use of various angles of shooting. Many actors have noted that, like a sticky cobweb in the corner of the mind, it is difficult to be unaware that as a beginning actor one is often shot from a less effective angle while the best angles are given to the more experienced actors. Occasionally, contracts made between agents and producers stipulate a certain number of shots for the actors represented. This kind of career insurance does not consider the artistic demands of the script, of course.

Sometimes the director may be fond of over-the-shoulder shots and use them excessively. In *Chapter Two*, for example, there are too many over-the-shoulder shots of James Caan as he watches and listens to Marsha Mason in her emotional driving scenes of determination to get their marriage working. In this context—the power of the Mason character's objective—these two-character shots dilute the characterization. James Caan's back becomes distressingly distracting. The spectator is jarred by not being able to concentrate solely on her. Although Caan executed these over-the-shoulder shots professionally, remaining still through them, the shots remain distracting. It is the quantity, not the quality, of shots that disturbs.

Pudovkin advised the actor to understand and feel the possibilities of shooting shots from various angles. In an over-the-shoulder shot, one must imagine the character at the corner of a frame, and respond in a more intimate and subdued manner, visualizing what it is like to catch a glimpse of someone out of the corner of your eye. Just as the stage actor knows when to use an emphatic gesture or hold a pause, so the film actor must become sensitive to the effect of certain angles and movements by the camera.

If, for example, the camera is tracking from above and behind the actor, and moves slowly, almost imperceptibly, to the front of the actor, level with his face, the general effect created in the spectator is anticipation. The viewer has been placed in the position of a voyeur, and "watches," eagerly awaiting the next action. The quality of the anticipation is determined by the circumstances surrounding the character—the spectator could be anxious, suspicious or concerned. The actor must be aware that whatever he does next, he is doing in the presence of a spectator who has been made ready to participate by the movement of the camera. If then the camera ends on a close-up of the actor's face, we expect to see the fullest nuance of whatever emotion the circumstances call for. It is time for the actor to give fully, unreservedly, whatever is needed at that moment. The film is running through the machine, and the actor should be prepared to give the maximum

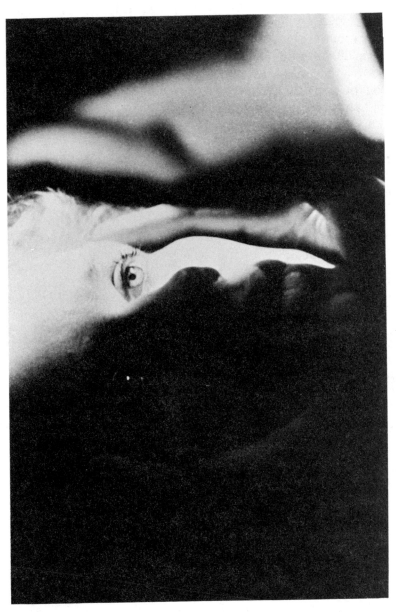

An extreme close-up of Liv Ullmann in Cries and Whispers.

expressiveness of that particular moment. Whatever the actor does should equal in stillness and intensity the quality of anticipation the camera has produced through its movement.

Because the film actor is limited in his choice of actions by the requirements of the camera, he should have a basic knowledge of the camera's technical aspects. The camera records both static and moving objects or persons. It organizes movement or a static picture within a frame and produces a series of images to engage the mind and imagination. Like the theatre, film work has a specific technical vocabulary which the actor should be familiar with. The bases of camera work presuppose an elementary knowledge of the terms defining the spatial relationship between the actor and the camera.

There are five basic types of shots in relation to distance:

- *Extreme close-up:* a camera shot which includes only a small portion of the actor's body (the eyes, hands, a part of his costume or props). This image will fill the screen.
- *Close-up:* a camera shot taken at close range which includes only a portion of the actor's body (his head and shoulders, for example).
- *Medium shot:* a camera shot that includes approximately half the subject (the actor's body from the waist up, for example).
- *Medium long shot:* a camera shot that includes the entire subject (the actor's body from head to toe).
- *Long shot:* a camera shot in which the focus of interest is a great distance from the camera. This shot may include many details of the environment in which the subject is filmed.

Very often, the director will shoot the entire scene in long shot. This is termed a *master or cover shot*. To the long shot will be added medium shots of the entire action, and medium close-ups of the critical action in the scene. The scene, then, is "covered" by filming it at various distances from the subject. It is essential that the action in each shot be as similar as possible to the action in the master shot (the long shot) to insure that there will be definite places for match-action cuts.

Two additional types of shots which the actor should know are the *cut-away shot* and the *reverse-angle shot*. In the cut-away shot, the camera films a subject that is not directly involved in the ongoing action. Usually, during long speeches of a character, the camera will cut away from the actor to another subject, which will relate in some way to what the actor is doing. For example, the actor is entering a strange house, speaking of the history of the families who lived there. The camera may cut away during the speech to framed photographs of the family members, or to a shot of adjoining rooms which the actor passes.

In the reverse-angle shot the action is shot from the opposite viewpoint of the original subject. Two actors are sharing a scene. In one shot the camera shoots over the shoulder of Character A, looking at Character B. This position will be reversed for the reverse-angle shot, over the shoulder of Character B, focusing on Character A. A reverse-angle shot is not always an over-the-shoulder shot, of course. By shooting the scene in reverse-angle, the director is getting both the action and the reactions of the characters. Many actors think it is an asset to characterization to be last in line for their reaction shots, because it gives them additional time to warm up to the scene, to find meaning in the action, to test various responses to the other characters. Since the actor does not have to carry the full responsibility of having the camera on him, he can listen more carefully to the other character and think through the implications of the action.

In addition to the kinds of shots basic to filmmaking, there are four basic angles:

- *Actor-level angle:* the camera is positioned in an angle parallel to the eye-level of the subject.
- *High angle:* the camera is positioned above the subject, looking downward.
- *Low angle:* the camera is positioned below the subject, looking upward.
- *Dutch angle:* any unusual position of the camera in relation to the subject.

CAMERA SETUP AND MOVEMENT

When an actor arrives for shooting, he will be filmed within a certain composition, and with or without movement of the camera. The construction of each shot in relation to the actor's position and

Actor-level angle shot of Carroll Baker in Baby Doll.

movement, and to the camera's position and movement, is called a "setup." The director and the cameraman collaborate on the setup. The decision on where to place the camera is based on such factors as whether the action takes place in the foreground or in depth, whether the camera will remain stationary or move. If the camera moves, the setup must accommodate the degree and direction of its movement. The setup, then, is a structure for the action within each shot, similar to the director's blocking or movement for a stage play.

Let us use a simple scene to illustrate the setup and its requirements upon the actor. Joe enters a restaurant, greets several of the customers, and then stops at one of the tables to say a line to Jane. As Joe speaks to Jane, we see the villain Jake, gun in hand, moving toward Joe. The scene will be shot in a subject-level angle by a stationary camera, in a medium shot.

Since the camera is stationary, Joe's movements are critical ones: his lines and actions must blend with Jake's movement. Joe must hit an exact mark at the table, for instance, so that when Jake moves closer to the table, the shot will contain all three characters in an arrangement that the director wishes to retain. Let us say that if Joe stops camera left of the table, the composition will include Jake in the background. If Joe moves too far camera right, his figure will obstruct a clear vision of Jake. For the actor playing Jake, this setup requires that he begin his walk toward Joe and Jane on a certain physical or verbal cue in the action in order to preserve the composition.

Now let us suppose the camera will move with Joe as he makes his cross from the door into the room and to the table. The camera will track in a parallel direction with Joe. An additional action is inserted by the director—a minor character in the scene will move in a direction opposite to Joe at a specific point in the action. The director also decides that the camera will crane upward, and shoot downward when Jake moves toward Joe. This time through Joe must hit his mark not only to keep the composition open, but also because he will be lit by a special lighting camera left of the table. The action, therefore, must be timed to allow the camera to move from a parallel tracking position to a crane position.

The setup is discussed with the actors to point out the logistics of the filming, and then the scene will be rehearsed several times before the cameras film the action. During the shooting Joe may drop the cue that the minor female character in the background uses for her cross. Joe may move too far camera right, obscuring Jake. Jake may begin to cross toward Joe too soon or too late. The special lighting may be too bright. The background female may forget to cross, even though the cue is given. The director at some point in this chaos will call for the action to be "cut;" everyone will move back to the pre-action positions, the director will repeat his directions for timing and movement, or make some adjustments in the directions. The key grip will adjust the lighting. After a brief pause to allow everyone to regain concentration, the director will call for the camera to "roll" and the action will begin again. Each time the shot is filmed, it is numbered as a take. When the director is satisfied, the take will become a print.

In a single setup there are many technical requirements for the actors to incorporate into their performance. One part of the mind concentrates on the technical cues; the rest focuses on the characterization and action.

Several basic camera movements record the actor's work and influence his performance. The camera can "pan," which means that it pivots along a horizontal plane. "Tilting" the camera indicates a vertical pivot. When the camera is in a "dolly" movement, it will move either toward or away from the subject. A "tracking" camera moves in a horizontal direction parallel to the subject. A "craning" movement of the camera is a parallel movement in a vertical direction.

Camera movements and angles produce certain effects in the spectator's perception of and empathy with the actors and the action. If the actor becomes aware of the camera movement used in a setup, he can either play with or against the effect of the camera's movement and angle. For instance, an upward tilt or angle of the camera usually emphasizes the dominance of the subject. It is an assertive movement and angle. The actor being shot in this way can choose to increase the effect of dominance through body posture or attention on small movements within the frame. This rapid concentration of attention can increase the tension of the scene, and give must be supported by the script.

A dolly movement, especially if short and quick, can focus our attention on small movements within the frame. This rapid concentration of attention can increase the tension of the scene, and give more significance to the movement. A dolly out from the subject can broaden the context of a gesture, increase the number of details we associate with the character, and change the rhythm of action in the scene. A dolly out from the actor can produce the same effect of involvement that is found in a musical composition when it moves from a note played by a single instrument to the many melodies of the full orchestra participating. An overused dolly out in film is one which moves from an actor-level position out to a camera position that looks downward from a great height upon the characters. Two lovers embracing, for instance, will appear caught in their own cocoon of emotion in the eye-level position when the camera is close to them. As the camera dollies out and moves upward, the lovers are expanded into symbols of love, happiness, and joy. Their individuality is lessened as they expand in this symbolic way to become surrogates for eternal love.

In a similar way the camera movement that tracks the action in a circular motion, as we see in the dancing scenes with Carrie and Tommy in *Carrie* and Agatha and Stanton in *Agatha*, seems to increase the concentration and isolation of the characters within their feelings, stretching the emotional aspects by making every second seem fuller and denser. This consequently slows down our perception of time.

The changing composition in a shot that a moving camera creates can produce changes in the emotional intensity of acting. A shot may have more or less tension depending upon the movement of the camera isolating or broadening gestures or action.

Every camera angle changes the composition within the space in which the action happens, and changes our perception of the event. Experienced actors collaborate with the camera's ability to alter perception, and establish mood and atmosphere by adjusting their behavior accordingly. When the camera is in close-up on two actors' faces during a quarrel, it creates a charged atmosphere. Actors' movements in this case must not be so charged with tension that, in conjunction with the camera, an exaggerated tension is established.

The kind and number of objects and settings in the shot also have an influence on the actor's performance. In *Agatha*, for example, many of Redgrave's early scenes as Agatha are shot in extremely low-level lighting. The settings include restricted areas: the engraver's shop, the narrow hallway outside her husband's office, and crowded streets and lobbies. This combination of low light and restricted environments enhances our perception of Agatha's tense demeanor, shyness and anxiety. We will carry this assessment of Agatha's temperament far into the story of the film.

The breakfast quarrel scene is shot in more spacious and brighter surroundings, encouraging the spectator to hope, as Agatha does, that the situation will be brighter as well. The juxtaposition of the setting and the action in this scene, when Agatha falls to her knees and begs her husband to stay, increases our empathy for her. This accumulation of images, light and dark, restricted and spacious, within certain contexts develops the characterization in the same manner as the actor's work. Redgrave's personal gestures as Agatha suit the environment in which the scenes take place. She is restrained and simple in the dark and crowded environments; open and more exuberant in the spacious and bright environment.

A deep-focus shot, in which we see many well-lit details of the setting that run from the foreground to the farthest limit of the background, offers more freedom to the actor. It allows him to move within a greater range. It permits more contact with the setting and props. It broadens the range of relationships and increases the environmental aspect of the image. The actor can relate to the reality of furniture, props, and walls—a relationship the stage actor finds both comforting and challenging.

Shots that are restricted by the spatial composition also restrict the degree and kind of actor movement. In Bernardo Bertolucci's *The Conformist*, the camera begins one scene with a medium shot of Dominique Sanda. She moves away from the camera towards the window at her left, then turns back toward the camera as it moves into a medium close-up of her. Sanda is joined in this shot by Jean-Louis Trintignant who appears from her left. They are both now in medium close-up of her. Sanda was required to hit a mark which would allow Trintignant to join her in the shot. The instant both actors are included in the shot, their movement is greatly restricted. When the camera remains stationary on them, it demands very selective gesture and expression since these movements are the only variables in the shot. At this range, and in this restricted space, any movement is significant.

A shot that limits gesture and expression is the close-up of an actor in a restricted environment, such as the shot of Vanessa Redgrave in Ken Russell's *The Devils*. In the film Redgrave plays a humpbacked nun whose soul is as deformed as her body. The particular shot in reference is a close-up view in which she looks up through a very small grated window at Grandier (Oliver Reed). In such a shot the actor must be careful not to overaccentuate the sense of confinement in the shot. The close-up, the grating, the size of the window are frame details that construct the image of confinement. If the actor overaccentuates the confinement, he embellishes that image but doesn't refine or deepen its meaning. Embellishment and adornment for their own sakes bring very little to the experience of an event.

Whenever the actor can, he should work within the limitations of the shot. In close-up or medium-shot work, the actor needs to simplify gesture and refine the subtlety of response. In long and deep-focus shots, the actor can find ways to use more of the entire body; he can relate to the environment that will be included in the shot.

9

THE ACTOR'S
TECHNIQUES

USE OF THE SELF: CONTACT
AND EXPRESSION

Acting, whether onstage or on the screen, is the creation of an image of character involved in a series of actions and circumstances which are given by the author and conveyed by the actor to the spectator. To create the image of character the actor uses his instruments: his voice, body, gestures, his emotional and kinetic responses. It is this use of personal attributes and responses that embodies character. The actor's goal, of course, is to convey a person who could conceivably exist in reality without resorting to clichéd interpretations. Through the use of inventive and original behavioristic detail, the actor tries to convey to the spectator a deeper understanding of the many facets of human character and motivation.

Whether the image of character is to be projected on the screen or inside the theatre, the actor's first stages of work are the same. In his creation of an image he fuses the filmmaker's planned elements of characterization with his own individuality. Within this fusion lie all the potentials of greatly imaginative characterization. If the actor has a firm understanding of the nature and effect of his own individuality, he can use himself to produce a truthful, creative and subtle characterization; or he can get in the way of it. "Know thyself" is still a primary responsibility for the actor, especially the screen actor. He must be as aware of his effect on film as he is of the effect of others around him, and of those whom he has seen on film.

An objective evaluation of the mechanics of his everyday behavior and spontaneous responses is necessary to isolate those gestures and body language which would get in the way of the characterization he is trying to develop. In a sense, the actor must be able to free himself from himself, and from whatever behavior, mannerism, or body language is part of his total effect upon others. Once the actor is free to choose *not to use* his own mechanics of being, he is then ready to draw upon his bank of emotional and physical experience.

How does an actor learn to contact himself, to draw upon any inner resource, to identify the "persona" he projects? The artistic sensitivity reflects a powerful response to persons, objects, or experiences, and includes the ability to recall those responses at will. The actor's job is to remain vulnerable to the situation or other characters, and to retain spontaneity, or a semblance of spontaneity. These two qualities—vulnerability and spontaneity—work hand-in-hand. If an actor remains vulnerable, that is, open to being affected by the stimuli, he has more access to spontaneous responses.

Vulnerability is an individual trait. It manifests itself in a vast range of degrees. Some of us are more vulnerable to events than others. Every film actor does not have the vulnerability of Liv Ullmann, nor would any film actor want to exchange his own degree and character of vulnerability for another's. Walter Matthau, Jack Lemmon, Stacy Keach, and Jack Nicholson have quite different traits of vulnerability that are projected by the camera. Vulnerability is a reflection of one's vision of the world. Each writer is reflected in the story he tells. Each actor in the degree of vulnerability he brings to a role. What is important is that all actors try to increase their degree of receptiveness to the world, while retaining the unique caliber of vulnerability.

To increase receptiveness an actor can train himself to:

• Make use of more opportunities to respond sensitively.
• Increase the number of activities in which he is interested or actively engaged. These require making a definite effort to see the world around him, and taking note of it.

• Collect and catalog human responses as treasures of possible characterization traits.

This doesn't mean that the actor should take his own emotional temperature twelve times a day. But like a person newly given sight, an actor must see things for the first time as often as possible. In fact, the actor must increase his sensitivity to stimuli affecting all five physical senses.

Our emotions are stored in our physical senses. This is why we often describe important events from the past in physical terms. In Rolfing therapy, manipulation of certain areas of the body will produce mental images of specific events from the individual's past. Acupuncture, a form of physical stimulation, can relieve pain. Our bodies are the reservoir of emotional memory. Anything physical the actor does, from meditation to active sports, will tune both his physical and emotional instrument.

Spontaneity is allied with intuition. Actors should exercise their intuitive capabilities. One way to free intuition is to use metaphors in response to the first reading of a script. For example, as an actor reads a script, he might find it useful to note any response to the character or action in simple terms of colors; in terms of weather conditions; or parallel experiences in the actor's life. Any analogies the actor makes will exercise his intuitive responses.

Spontaneity or the appearance of spontaneity is an essential ingredient in film acting. Most film actors facing the pressure of many takes and long waits between takes discover that maintaining spontaneity is one of the most difficult tasks they have. Responses must not look fixed or planned; they must seem to occur in the moment.

This phrase "in the moment" is a helpful one for actors to use. Using the moment-to-moment technique doesn't mean relying upon sudden inspiration. The technique requires disciplining one's self to become involved in the action each time it is performed. Sudden inspirations are the result of the artist's doing some particular and specific action which touches a specific emotional memory, and automatically engages his entire physical, mental, and emotional modes of being.

Imagine the billions of pathways in the brain. At various

points along these pathways are stored our experiences. We do not yet know exactly how the brain works or how to control our brain waves. There are as yet no channel markers that we can use to lead us instantaneously to a specific memory or feeling. However, we can enter this realm of recall through meditation on the physical elements surrounding the event.

Inspiration has much in common with another type of common experience: we see a particular kind of object in a particular setting (a grove of birch trees, a battered shoe); we notice a particular aroma in some setting; we hear a particular piece of music—and suddenly we are in the midst of re-experiencing an event from our past. No amount of planning can arouse that event or the re-experience of it. Some combination of stimuli provokes it, catches us off-guard and plants us in the middle of the event.

Although the actor hopes for inspiration to come, he cannot guarantee its arrival. He can, however, achieve spontaneity in several ways: concentrating on a new metaphorical image, distracting himself from the techniques he has accumulated over the years of work, playing the scene without all the answers, or with no answers. No actor succeeds in achieving spontaneity in every single take. The loss of spontaneity in the repetition of takes is an occupational hazard in film work. Worry about it causes both inspiration and spontaneity to run for cover. Both elements only exist in a free, and relaxed atmosphere and attitude.

Life and experience shape our physical character and personality as individuals. We develop automatic gestures through which we express some aspect of self. These automatic gestures are often unconscious ones. Observe a contestant on a TV quiz show, or in a beauty contest, and you find such unconscious gestures expressing the stress of the situation: licking the lips, quivering mouth, fingers toying with the hair, straightening clothing. Every person has a repertoire of these automatic gestures. The actor may have two sets of these automatic gestures: one set that he uses in life and a second set that he uses as an actor. For example, an actor may use his voice to attract attention as well as communicate the character's needs. There is a double intention heard in the voice, and it may confuse the spectator. The actor must become aware of both sets of automatic gestures. He does not have to get rid of them, but he must be able to control them, to choose when to use them and when not to use them.

Some of these automatic gestures are closely linked to personality and can be assets. Jack Lemmon's tendency to stammer in scenes of conflict is an example of an automatic gesture that is a characterizing trait for his screen personality as well. Al Pacino tends to look at the actor speaking to him for a few beats, and then shifts his eyes in another direction. Pacino uses this gesture while listening and as he speaks—as though his next thought or idea is located somewhere in space to the left or right of him.

One distracting automatic gesture is the tendency of an actor to rely totally on himself for emotional stimuli, ignoring the most important stimulus he has as an actor—the other actors. Automatic gestures can be expressed in a physical mannerism, a vocal or speech characteristic, or an attitudinal posture. They are neither bad nor good in themselves. Only if they detract from the actor's communication ability should they be eliminated from his work.

Before concentrating on lifelike acting, the film actor must analyze the nature and quality of his automatic gestures, and he must also know what psychological, physical, and social traits are inherent in himself as projected by the camera. To do this he must pay close attention to what qualities other actors project on film, and how his own differ. Any film actor should use those elements of his personality which are especially communicative on film. The theatre actor must learn how to put himself in touch with himself through exercises in concentration, relaxation, and improvisation. The film actor must not only accomplish that honesty of behavior, but also must come into contact with his screen self. He must discover whether his is visually or aurally oriented. The sound of truthful behavior cannot be imitative on film. When the camera focuses in on a close-up of the face, looking a certain way at another character to communicate a need cannot be falsified. The film actor must become an expert in truthful behavior before he begins to layer on character traits.

Since a major quality of film is the physical, and since the actor's physical presence has an identity from which you cannot stray too far, the film actor must train himself to analyze his personal methods of coping with events and situations in life, combining it with an awareness of both his emotional and physical reactions. For automatic gestures are not confined to physical gestures. Certain physical gestures are organic to each person's response to certain situations. If the actor is unaware of his own physical responses, he is unable *not* to use them in his creation of character. These personal physical responses—perhaps a certain tilt of the head when an actor listens to another person or a toying with the buttons on his shirt when the actor is insecure—must be noted by the actor as organic to himself. While useful in one role, they may be distracting in another.

Sandy Dennis is one film actor who is overloaded with psychophysical gestures. She appears at times in her early films unable to communicate at all without blinking her eyes, twitching her jaw, or waving her hand, index finger pointing. Many critics of her early films felt she was acting with every part of her body, each one doing its own acting, all at the same time. In Dennis' case, her physical mannerisms did more than establish a screen persona—they dissipated the effect of that identity. This hand-acting and rubbery face-pulling seem to be common among many young actresses who play the shy, sensitive, victimized roles. Dennis' physiognomy in action seemed like a glass about to shatter, a wall about to topple. As the betrayed wife in Alan Alda's *The Four Seasons*, Dennis was perfect. Her mannerisms suited the nervous, anxious woman who was struggling through a mid-life crisis. At the same time, we could sympathize with the husband who left her. Anyone would find it difficult to cope with such a hyperactive spouse. Alda's script supported the mannerisms Dennis uses. It identified her as a woman whose decisions about what to do with her life were as scattered as her dissipating gestures.

Automatic gestures can also be found in internal actions of the human psyche. For example, when challenged either in life or within a scripted scene, an actor may respond out of a superior attitude, covering and camouflaging his real feelings. When given a compliment in life, or on screen, an actor may tend to respond automatically with a grin or a sarcastic remark. Sometimes the actor's automatic internal gestures or postures may suit the character; often they will not. Again, the actor must be aware of his organic response, and consciously elect to use it or change it for the character.

Since these gestures are often a way to cope with positive or negative stress and are acquired habits, they can frequently be totally wrong for the character. In that circumstance, their use can affect the actor's credibility as a believable character. When watching a Faye Dunaway performance, we sometimes feel that what we are seeing is an idea of an image that Dunaway or her directors feel is striking enough to hold our attention on its own. Often it is not.

Believability is essential to the film actor's craft. In fact, one might stress it as the foundation of film acting. Without its presence in characterization, we see only phoniness or symbolic acting, indicating emotion and action, but not recreating it. "Indicating" is the substitution of a recognized physical emblematic action for the simple execution of a motivated action. For example, an actor supposedly listening for a sound will *indicate* listening by cocking his head this way or that way. The body goes through the emblematic motions of listening, but the actor is not himself involved in listening. Indicating is a sign language of acting. It doesn't work because the audience can witness the disengagement or overexertion of the actor at work. To illustrate indicating to a beginning actor, find a person who does not play piano well, but can read notes. Ask that person to play a difficult piece on the piano, and observe her. She will be fully concentrated on playing the music. Then ask another actor to recreate her difficulty. The second actor will often indicate the difficulty by overkill. The hand movements will be exaggerated, the facial frustration will be too much; the second actor will exert too much effort in showing us the frustration.

Believability results when the actor performs the action simply, with a motivation or justification, and with a sense of exploration underlying the action. In the piano-playing exercise, the first actor was trying hard to make the connection between the musical notes she read and the dexterity of her fingers. Her main focus was on this mental action. Trying to play was the important action. The second actor tried to show us how the hands made mistakes, but the mental action of wanting to make the connection was missing.

The finest film actors *seem* to be living the action and experiencing the consequences from moment to moment. In film, believability is such a critical factor for success that one rarely sees an indicating actor. In *Tarzan the Ape Man*, Bo Derek not only indicated her action, but also posed and postured throughout the film.

The film actor must resolve to be simple, to do things simply, and to believe in the actions. He must find motivations to justify his actions, even the simplest tasks such as entering a building.

FILM CHARACTERIZATION

Imagination and observation are two basic elements of development for film characterization. Observation of others often leads us to make certain conclusions about their personalities, their character attributes and flaws, and their actions. Conscious observation can give us exact information about characterization. In the piano exercise, the second actor will generally overcome that tendency to indicate by watching the first actor play the piano, and then by trying to recreate exactly what he has observed the first actor doing. No more and no less.

The conclusions we make about others based on our observation of them may be clichéd, or they may be creative and inventive. An obese person is not always cloddish; a thin person not always anxious or tense. Zero Mostel and John Belushi amaze audiences with their light and graceful movement. The actor must learn to collect physical data related to behavior, and to execute the physical movement, trying it out in his own body. He should catalog for future use the ways in which people walk and talk and the styles of clothing various people wear at work or play. The actor should build a storehouse of character references based on his observations of life in art, history, politics, family dynamics, and love. In order for these collections of observations to be made believable, the actor must execute them. Doing them, using them, stretches the actor's creativity and develops his skill.

When the actor begins his approach to a characterization, he first defines the character's actions and situations and finds ways to embody those actions, both mental and emotional, in a believable manner. The camera will magnify any artificiality, and consequently the bond between actor and spectator is disrupted. It is not necessary for an actor to "feel" the emotion. If the actor concentrates simply on doing the action, the corresponding emotion will be called forth. The problem of acting lies in achieving the

Steve McQueen as Dr. Stockmann in An Enemy of the People.

simplicity of action which is necessary to unlock these emotional impulses—nothing must interfere in the flow or impede its progress.

Character actors like Dustin Hoffman, Maggie Smith, James Mason, and Shelley Winters transform their personal identities into the specific identities required by the script. A character actor must filter the written characteristics through his own person; and, via himself-as-actor, exist in the specific circumstances. In film it is very difficult to become other than yourself, since the camera so readily identifies the personality. Can an actor apply makeup and convey character as vividly as some of Fellini's "naturals" (non-actors)? The director using these naturals has the advantage, since the camera records not only the externals of personality, but also all the internal, usually unconscious, facets of the psyche. Modern character actors come very close to achieving a degree of transformation that submerges their personal identities. Dustin Hoffman as Ratso in *Midnight Cowboy*, James Mason in *Lolita*, Peter Sellers in *Being There*, Gena Rowlands in *Gloria*, and Simone Signoret in *Madame Rosa* are highlight events in the history of actor transformation. Beneath such successes in acting is actor research and study.

For *Midnight Cowboy*, Hoffman found an old, battered raincoat in a shop, and wore it on the streets, frequenting the kinds of places that the character Ratso would frequent. In this activity Hoffman absorbed the milieu of the movie and transformed himself into the character. Director John Schlesinger, who accompanied Hoffman on some of these forays, was astonished to note how completely Hoffman seemed to blend into the environment, becoming one with it. Observation of others has always been a critical element in the training of actors. Hoffman enriched his observation by his own physical participation, feeding and nourishing his imagination.

Imagination is not a mystical movement of the mind which suddenly gives birth to a new idea. Imagination must be nourished by observation and experience. It is a facility of the mind to create new ideas by combining elements of other ideas or objects, and fashioning them in a new context. Imagination is a kind of sculpture wherein the mind uses materials from many disparate sources to build new forms of ideas. Dreams offer the most information about how imagination works in its combination of

Dustin Hoffman and Jon Voight in Midnight Cowboy.

dissimilar objects or ideas. The dream mechanism taps the infinite possibilities of combinations. Dreams are metaphors. These metaphorical substitutions and visual analogies offer striking information about the world and our experiences in it.

Like a poet or painter, the actor must observe the world around him—its people, its objects, its mysteries—and use this material in the creation of character, human action and behavior. The character of Chance Gardiner, played by Peter Sellers in *Being There*, was himself like an actor at work. Chance Gardiner put together a persona constructed from elements that the character observed on television: a way to shake hands, a way to kiss and embrace, a way to address a president, etc. Through observation and imagination, actor Peter Sellers fashioned the character Chance Gardiner who created a personality out of the bits and pieces of human behavior he observed on television. It's also interesting that the physical demeanor of Chance Gardiner encouraged others to take him for a wise man. In actuality, the character Chance is illiterate, and close to moronic.

Observation, then, is an important tool for the actor. He should develop the habit of doing "homework" for each role he plays by making the effort to observe in life the milieus and behavior patterns which suit the individual characters he creates. Gena Rowlands in *Gloria* brought a metropolitan toughness to Gloria; she looked natural in the garish wardrobe Gloria favored. Rowlands endowed Gloria with a "big-city hide"—harassed, outspoken, direct, quick, and no-nonsense. Bertolt Brecht commented when working on a film with Joseph Losey that, "To me one of the major jobs of the actor is to observe all the time. . . . in fact a hundred observations from which to draw until he gets one that fits. Fits because he feels right doing it, or because the director says that it's right and incorporates it into his performance." Observing human nature and collecting usable details will build the storehouse of character detail which can express in surprising and illuminating ways the internal action of the character.

The actor need not look only for bizarre or extraordinary detail in observing others. Everyday behavior of people around us provides a wealth of interesting detail. Watch someone tap a friend on the shoulder. The turn and expression of surprise of the one tapped will convey various kinds of information. People waiting in lines register varying sorts of impatient behavior. Ask yourself how you know someone feels slighted by another, or is hesitant to answer a certain question. What happens to the face or body that informs you of feelings and emotions? Physical behavior is a packaging of the inner life.

In order to produce interesting behavior for the camera, the actor must concentrate on three elements of characterization: the internal, the external, and transformation.

The first work will be to gauge and analyze the internal life of the character, becoming familiar with the inner mechanisms of the character, his motivations, his intentions, his objectives, his needs and desires. The quality of life that the character lives has an effect upon his internal characteristics. For the actor to portray the character accurately, he must fully relate to the scope of this internal life. The range and depth of the character's intelligence, his thought-making processes, his decision-making abilities, are all part of the internal characteristics.

Determining the internal qualities of the character is essential to the actor's preparation for characterization. Thought should be given to several areas in relation to the character.

How strong is the character's will to live? Does the character grow or develop? Where, how, which scenes, what kind of change? If there is no essential development, what qualities are revealed during each scene? What is the character's point of view toward life, toward others? Is the character fighting his environment? Does the character form ideas quickly? These types of questions are by no means the only way to determine character. Actors respond creatively to other means of finding character: sounds, colors, and images.

Brando's characterization of the "regulator" in *The Missouri Breaks* was stimulated by Arthur Penn's description of the image he had for the character: ". . . a kind of hermit crab. He goes into an area and inhabits someone's shell for a while, consumes everything around there, and then moves on to another shell." This ruthlessness was incorporated into Brando's characterization as we see it on the screen. There was also much in the characterization of the Indian's close ties with the earth, of being stabilized by the contact between one's feet and the ground beneath them.

A specific internal orientation will allow the actor to react appropriately to whatever situations are presented during the scenes. The actor doesn't need to preplan any reactions. And indeed, the actor should not preplan any response. Many actors insure a spontaneous, organic response by not learning the lines. Marcello Mastroianni, for instance, doesn't always learn his lines when working with Fellini on a film. Mastroianni tries to know exactly what kind of person the character is, and then lets Fellini tell him *what* to say as they shoot. Through this technique, both Fellini and Mastroianni strive to make everything happen naturally, convincing the audience of the spontaneity.

Every action, response, feeling, and emotion should evolve out of the moment in time *during shooting*. This is not easy because repeating the scene during rehearsals and shooting may cause responses to grow stale. What can the actor do? He can alter his response during each rehearsal and take, testing each one for all its images of truth in behavior. George Cukor and other directors advise their actors to vary the intentions and motivations every time for every take, to introduce changes in the way the character does things for each take. The actor can concentrate on the other actors, looking for new aspects in their characterizations which may evoke a more imaginative response in him.

The internal characteristics should have a form which includes the way the person dresses, walks, talks, looks at others, listens to others, expresses ideas, or copes with conflict. The function of such external form is to communicate instantly the kind of person the filmgoer is watching. Since film communicates the smallest movement so vigorously, all movement selected by the actor to express the form must be distinct, subtle, and imaginative.

Marlon Brando's entrance in *The Missouri Breaks* is an imaginative external choice. As he approaches the house and greets the young independent woman, he hangs from an upside-down position on his horse. Immediately the gesture characterizes him as a man who will put others into a position of never knowing what he will do next. So while his smile seems a welcoming grin, his capricious behavior carries an element of danger. Later this hired killer plies his fatal trade wearing the bonnet, apron, and long skirt of a homesteading woman. The outer garb of a sacrificing pioneer female stuns the spectator by the macabre connection with an unconscionable murderer. These selections could not be more distinct and imaginative.

Brando does not generalize a character. In the act of killing, the character has a work-a-day attitude much like a factory technician on an assembly line. The internal orientation towards taking a life is the same he might give to examining the skies for rain clouds. Add to this the Irish brogue Brando uses, and you have a most unconventional portrayal of a hired killer.

In choosing physical, social, and psychological traits for character, the actor should always put a great value on the element of surprising juxtaposition. The selection of traits should be powerful and engaging in their visual and auditory content. It is through the visual and auditory images that we engage in the character's activity. In a more recent film, *The Formula*, Brando plays a wealthy amoral tycoon. His fully packed frame smartly adorned, he is the essence of American capitalism. The performance is a delightful mixture of opposites, a Brando signature on a role. One of the last gestures Brando makes in *The Formula* is to offer his enemy a "Milk Dud." The villain is not taking candy from a baby, but offering candy to a baby. This reversal has a sinister comedy.

Other film performances with imaginative selection of external traits are those of Robert Duvall in *The Great Santini* and Peter Sellers in *Being There*.

Duvall creates a dynamic portrait of a "gung-ho dinosaur," a "warrior without a war," the bragging soldier who dominates the family circle, infecting each member with anger as well as love. Duvall uses a rigid Marine posture and proud stride carried to extremes. His voice is loud and commanding. The laugh and grin are so engaging that one immediately likes this overbearing "Bull" and can forgive his failings as a father, husband, and Marine. He can be a nasty cheat who plays dirty in a basketball game with his son, yet the pride in his eyes when he speaks of his son's birth communicates a gentle affection.

Sellers' choice of makeup for Chance Gardiner is stylized: pale complexion with heavy lines outlining the eyes, particularly the lower lids of the eyes in a Chaplinesque fashion. His walk and gestures are contained within a limited space, as though Sellers

Brando as tycoon Adam Steiffel in The Formula. *Brando never plays one thing only in a character. There are always many facets of personality revealed.*

may have imagined the character enclosed within a box. He relates to the world as though it were all a program on television. The internal characterization includes the following traits: a naivete, a direct response to others with little subtext, an energetic concentration on everything that happens to him or around him.

The selection of internal and external traits is a conscious, thoughtful act of the artist. Without selection, art is a "happy accident." The actor may be lucky enough to fall into a perfect characterization for the role once or twice. The serious film actor learns to do his work on every role.

Transformation into the character demands discipline and hard work. Like imagination, transformation must be nourished by other elements. Gathering and selecting the internal and external details of character provides the material for the actor's transformation into the character. It is then the actor's work to absorb these details and use them naturally.

Sally Field in *Norma Rae* convinces us that she is a factory worker in several ways: she wears functional clothing; she responds in a functional rather than intellectual manner. She is coarse around the edges. The reticence and restraint of the intellectual is replaced with a freedom of enjoyment in living. There is a down-to-earth quality about the way she does everything. The method of executing the action defines the character. Transformation means the actor has given over his psyche and his physical being to the character *with no reservations*. The work of transformation begins with the first reading of the script when one or two of the character's actions or traits "touch" the actor. This empathetic response starts the wheels of the acting machine rolling. Although the actor may not think consciously again about his responses to the first reading, he will be affected by it. Further readings of the script tend to intensify the empathetic response and encourage the actor to select details which will embody the character.

The unconscious mind as well as the conscious mind is at work on the transformation through discussions with the director, through rehearsals, through selection of costume and makeup.

Working on the wardrobe and makeup for the character is a key element in the transformation. The actor must beware of choosing a hairstyle, makeup, or wardrobe because it makes him look good. The important question is whether it suits the character. The actor's ego may tug at him, while the character's needs also demand physicalization.

Donald Sutherland is an actor whose characterizations reveal a careful selection of wardrobe and costume, as well as an acquiescence to character needs over personal ones. Sutherland's hairstyles have included a curly perm (*Don't Look Now*), a no-part style in which the hair is combed straight back from the forehead (*The Eagle Has Landed*), and an elongated forehead, with the hairline pushed very far back *(Casanova)*.

The change in an actor's hairstyle need not be as drastic as those of Sutherland's characters, but every actor ought to consider the benefits towards transformation that these kinds of imaginative decisions can offer. A choice of hairstyle is only one of the decisions an actor makes. The body's configuration can be altered with slight padding or by the style of the clothing. The first time an actor sees himself in costume and makeup is another plateau in the journey towards transformation. This event is an opportunity for the actor to relate to the character. Conscious and unconscious processes are at work as the actor communes with his altered state as he looks in the mirror. Taking the time to respond to this new image is a fruitful exercise. The physical configuration and adornment of the body create a marked trail into the inner action of character.

For work in historical films or westerns, the actor should supplement whatever information the script gives with his own research into the period. The manner of speech and movement is an outgrowth of the political, social, and environmental aura of a particular period. Actors in period costumes must physically seem products of the time, not modern actors who just happen to be wearing period costumes. An actor's observation of any period should include studies of paintings of the times, social and cultural histories, music, and mores. As there is a collective unconscious among those living in any one era, so there is a collective knowledge. The actor must try to digest the collective knowledge of the era in which the movie is set and behave accordingly.

Whatever behavioral action the actor layers over himself in his characterization should become for him organic actions, not interrupted by any other consciousness. His choices of a new breathing rate, facial movement, explanatory gesture, intonations of words,

Donald Sutherland in Fellini's Casanova.

handling of objects, and bodily movements are part of the external forms through which he will express the inner workings of the character.

Anthony Hopkins as Sir Frederick Treves in *The Elephant Man* gives an excellent example of vocal virtuosity. He must give a complicated medical explanation of John Merrick's physical condition in highly technical language. He handles the terms as though they were second nature, which they would be to a medical person. While Hopkins rattles off the technical vocabulary, he also actively plays his objective: to impress the significance of his medical find on his colleagues. In order for Hopkins to succeed in this characterization, he must first have absorbed the medical vocabulary before he could add the playing of objectives.

Some external traits are demanded by the script, such as expert technical familiarity or equestrian skills. Some externals are invented by the actor, such as Sellers' walk, or Brando's greeting from the upside-down position. Whichever source the external trait springs from, it must be absorbed by the actor as though it were second nature.

If believability is the warp and the woof of film acting, then subtlety is the finest "thread passing through the warp." In film, subtlety is the skill of doing the least one can do to make a fine distinction in the meaning of the action.

What we respond most to in film is the expressive face—one able to register the subtle nuances of emotion and thought as well as the general outline. The face need not be handsome or beautiful, but it must be expressive. The actor working for subtlety and nuance hopes to build the skill of suggesting the tiniest movement of the inner life with the least amount of self-consciousness. Greta Garbo and Liv Ullmann are esteemed for their abilities to register thought with the least amount of movement. Everything seems to take place within the eyes.

Because the camera is so precise an observer, subtle movement of any internal or external action is essential. If one glances right or left, one cannot do so in an obvious manner; if one listens, one cannot do anything more than is necessary to listen, which means that one need only make the decision to listen for some sound or to another's work. Listening is a mental action in combination with

Dustin Hoffman's Ratso in Midnight Cowboy.

the engaged hearing mechanism of the ear. Make the decision to listen, allow the face to be still, and you will have listening that is precise.

A film actor who is not subtle will:

- show you what he is supposed to be doing
- overdo the action
- embellish the action or response with unnecessary movements either of the body or the mind.

The craft of subtlety in film acting demands that an actor's movements be somewhat slower and more contained than comparable actions in a theatre. The camera, especially in a close-up, emphasizes size and alters our perception of the tempo of movement. Acting in close-up should contain slightly slower movement in order for the spectator to follow the logic of thought beneath the action. The exaggeration in size also emphasizes the slightest movement, making it *appear* to be a bigger, faster motion.

In long shots, movement can be executed in normal tempo, since the actor is only a small part of the frame detail. The camera can follow his motion as he remains fixed in the frame. Different camera angles can either intensify or diminish the perception of motion within the frame. Since the actor has little or no control over the angles used, and sometimes has no knowledge of which take and angle will be used in the final print, he would benefit by slowing down his movement, and limiting the amount of movement he makes during a close-up.

While subtlety is the skill of doing as little as necessary to convey meaning, nuance is the coloring of the action. Nuance adds gradations of meaning to the action, whether it is spoken or physical. Subtlety in acting before the camera can be learned, primarily through practice in toning down the style of movement and increasing the conversational quality in the spoken word. Nuance in characterization must first be experienced or observed with a sensibility that responds to the variations of meaning in human action.

Nuance provides the surprising gesture, the uncommon reaction. Nuance builds layers of meaning, and like chiaroscuro in painting, through slight additions or subtractions, it adds variations to responses. Instead of the broad, flat outline of characterization found in one-layered performances, the performance of nuance creates a mist through which one can pick out many elements of character. It creates an elusive character, one whose reactions are multi-dimensional.

Actors seeking to supply a characterization with some nuances should concentrate not on the obvious responses to circumstances, but on the infinite possibilities of response to any stimuli. For example, every positive action has a negative counterpart. Faith exists because doubt is overcome . . . for the moment. Every act of faith, whether it's related to loving, trusting, having confidence, or making a thoughtful decision, rests precariously on its foundation. Beneath the surface of the foundation lies a magma of doubt, fear, suspicion, embarrassment, hesitation, ad infinitum. The actor playing a complex moment of human action must decide whether to reveal both the positive and negative aspects of the moment in order to add nuance to the characterization. James Mason in *Lolita* created a performance unequalled in nuance. His characterization of the intellectual Humbert Humbert, swathed in a seedy psychology, never fails to surprise, repulse, delight, and disgust.

Another clue to nuance is the sense of mystery and ambiguity created by the actor. The character constantly surprises us, gives us insights into behavior and sings the melodies of the soul. Nuance springs from a knowledge of human psychology. Nuances in the role are achieved when the actor plays against the obvious reactions. Not every sadness is relieved by tears; there are sadnesses too grievous for tears. Not every joy is expressed through smiles; there are joys too glorious for smiles. In *Agatha*, when Stanton asks Agatha for a kiss, Redgrave plays all the nuances of the progression of feelings and thoughts in the way she looks at Stanton. In her face we see annoyance at his forwardness, coupled with perplexity over why he should find her attractive, as well as a slight apprehension over her own developing attraction to him. No one thought remains long on her face and in her eyes before another nuance in attitude takes over. These two critical qualities—subtlety and nuance—can both be developed through the actor's receptivity to variations in human behavior. They are linked to film characterization both as technique and art. The dedicated film actor will master the technique and transform it into art. Peter Brook describes Jeanne Moreau's acting as being an "endless series of tiny surprises." In

Glenda Jackson dances with the bulls in Ken Russell's Women in Love.

human nature there is an endless series of spontaneous emotional reactions and physical responses which are more curious than any an actor might invent.

At the end of the film *Elizabeth R*, Glenda Jackson, in the role of Elizabeth, uses a gesture which is incredibly surprising and yet so correct for the complex character of this queen. As she waits for death, she sits up in a chair (after having stood up for countless hours) and places a finger inside her mouth along the gum line. The camera remains on her in this position for many seconds. The gesture is a peculiar one, totally surprising in a queen, and consequently a powerful image for a dying queen no longer powerful. In one of the final shots, she takes her finger out, looks at it, and puts it back in her mouth. In this one strong gesture, Jackson has found an unforgettable metaphor for the need for comfort in the face of the final insult, and for the desire to take one's emotional temperature in the midst of crisis, and for the catastrophic truth that no matter what one is in life, in the throes of death, one is a human body.

AIDS TO CHARACTERIZATION

All of the actor's work must culminate in these strong physical images for the character. The actor can also turn to literature for graphic descriptions of behavior. In his novel *Buddenbrooks*, Thomas Mann writes scores of passages describing physical manifestations of personality, all of which could be useful to the actor in his study of human behavior. For instance, these descriptions of members of a wealthy burgher family might become the basis for character gesture: "Then he takes out his eye-glasses (he always wears three of them, on long cords that are forever getting tangled up in his white waistcoat) and sticks them on his nose, which he wrinkles up to make them stop on, and looks at me with his mouth open . . ." or "Tony was silent a moment, drying her tears. She carefully breathed on her handkerchief and pressed it against her eyes to heal their inflammation." or ". . . a little fat elderly lady in a Turkey shawl . . . was choosing a pot of flowers, examining, smelling, criticizing, chattering, and constantly obliged to wipe her mouth with her handkerchief." In these descriptive words the actor has a second-to-second breakdown of the activity, very important to consider when one has a specific amount of time in which to execute the action. If a director is going to use 25 feet of 35mm film in shooting a sequence, the actor has approximately 16 seconds to complete the action. Descriptions from the work of Thomas Mann, or from Ross MacDonald's *The Blue Hammer* ("But her eyes were in long focus now, looking back over the continent of her life."), give the actor specific work to do, and can be applied to various sorts of roles. As an actor becomes more proficient in recreating though his own body the descriptions of novelists, he will find it easier to fill screen time with interesting behavior.

Improvisation is an effective aid to characterization if the actor avoids any stereotyped responses to the situations. In rehearsal improvisations, it is important to give the other actors something which will surprise them, stimulating them to respond in a new, perhaps more subtle way. Finding new ways to receive, assimilate, and respond to the material of the scene, to the conflict and action, are part of the actor's work. The actor must fully explore each of these three areas of receptivity, assimilation, and response. The absence or interrupted action of one area will break the pattern of believability. The actor who "acts in a vacuum," uncolored by what the other characters say or do to him, will soon bore the audience.

Improvisations can also bring out the meaning of the lines and the action. Their use can investigate whether the lines are direct expressions of emotions, or a way to conceal the feelings. For an improvisation to work, the actor should intellectually understand the character's background, emotional makeup, social position, economic standing, inner drives, and external manifestations. From this base the actor relates to each improvisation, having imagined a number of ways the character could react.

When John Huston was asked in an interview what attributes characterized a fine film actor, he included the following: the shading an actor gives a line; his timing; his control; his knowledge of the camera; his relationship to the camera.

The shading an actor gives a line must be organic to some

inner shading of emotion that prompts the line. If the shading is only technically produced by the voice, the effect on screen is a hollow one. The actor seems like a beautifully constructed house, but with nobody home.

Timing can refer to the actor's ability to space the words and action to suit the distance and time allowed by the camera. If the actor must enter a room, cross behind a sofa, and sit next to another character, he must be able to space out the words in his text to suit that action. Obviously he does not enter, say the words and then do the action, but must coordinate the lines to the action. He may be able to find a place to pause, insert a gesture, and make it to the final mark on the sofa where the director needs him. Such timing requires an ability to speed up some action, or slow down other action or words in order to get the most into the few seconds available.

Timing also refers to the inner rhythms inherent in the progress of emotion and action. All emotion has a rhythm, a logical progression from one degree to the next. The actor who has a natural instinct for timing will follow all the degrees. Some actors will skip or jump from one degree to another, missing several steps in between. They may be too afraid to allow the emotion to follow its course. Just as an actor can rush his lines, so can he rush his feelings, clouding the reality of his action. The actor must learn to "let it happen" without interference from himself.

From a general idea of the kind and type of person the character is, the actor moves to a more specific analysis of the character's needs, and finally to an understanding of the *obstacles* preventing the character from attaining his objectives or fulfilling his needs. Introducing the obstacle into one's acting work enriches and deepens the interpretation of character. For Chance Gardiner in *Being There*, every experience presents an obstacle. Sellers played the obstacles in detail. In his conversation with Richard Basehart (as the Russian dignitary) Sellers' Chance almost tries to read lips to comprehend the meaning of simple words. He smiles if the Russian smiles. He imitates the behavior he observes, whether he sees it on television or in another person. In another scene between Chance and a black medical technologist, Gardiner tries to decide whether the technician is "Raphael" or might know "Raphael," for whom Gardiner has a message. In a very few eye glances, Sellers reveals a struggle with a faulty logic:

- A black man gave me a message for Raphael.
- All black men know Raphael.
- This black man might know who Raphael is. He might even be Raphael.

Only after meeting these obstacles in his thought processes, does Gardiner ask the question, "Do you know Raphael?"

A character who appears bored cannot be realistically played until the actor realizes that boredom is not a passive state. Action and obstacles to the action are involved: the bored person seeks to be amused, and can't be, wishes to become interested in something to relieve his inertia, and finds nothing will work. In order for the acting to be effective the actor must play both states, rather than just the end result of a bored attitude. A non-listening character must be seen deciding not to listen. A sobbing character has already lost the struggle. The more interesting action is to try *not* to cry; the struggle against the inclination to cry is active. Sobbing releases the tension immediately; the scene is over. The actor must not only play what his character wants, but also must play the conflicts which prevent the character from getting what he wants. Conflict is the core of creative action.

Any type of conflict must be embodied in physical gesture. For the film actor whose image of character will be projected in a series of brief shots and varied angles, it is important to find the right subtle gestures which will project elements of character and conflict quickly and imaginatively. In *Rachel, Rachel,* Joanne Woodward hitches down her girdle or underpants as she walks off to school. Immediately this characterizes her. By selecting a gesture most women would do in private, and using it in a public situation, Woodward imbues Rachel with a naivete. We also see Rachel look around, as though unconcerned, to check whether anyone's noticed her. The audience stores up this information and carries it along to the next scene, where they are better prepared to be given more information about the character.

Unless the actor knows the total effect of the character he plays, he is unlikely to be able to analyze the moment-to-moment rhythms of the character's actions. These physicalizations of conflict are the staples of film acting. Once the actor has determined the overall view of his character, he must evoke these obstacles to the character's desires and needs. He must look for opportunities to give the character over to a duality of purpose and intention, to embody the struggle for life beneath the form of the character. It is far more interesting to see struggle within the character than to watch an unobstructed inner action.

Having seen Woodward's character as a person who is uncomfortable in clothing, we see a later scene that reveals her discomfort within. Rachel is serving snacks to her mother's friends. Her external form—the gestures and childlike intonations—seems to be calling for parental approval, while on her face is revealed the self-disgust and controlled resentment she feels about responding in this childlike way. These qualities all come through simultaneously. While we observe one quality or trait, we intuit the other and then see it bleeding through to the surface. This makes the character complex and encourages the aware spectator to respond more complexly.

In *Last Tango in Paris*, Marlon Brando projected a complicated study of a man who had been hurt by the infidelity of his wife. Most critics preferred to concentrate only on one aspect of his portrayal—the character's sexual response to his pain—and to see the film merely as an exploration of disembodied sexuality. The look on Brando's face when he noticed the neighbor wearing an exact copy of his own bathrobe was fleeting and subtle, yet not only communicated his realization that this man was his wife's lover but also his decision to hide that recognition and the pain it caused. In *Agatha*, Vanessa Redgrave's response to Nancy Neele's line, "Shall I cancel everything?", conveys in one glance lasting no more than five seconds of screen time that she suspects Neele of having an affair with her husband.

The film actor must explore what Pudovkin calls "realisticness"—truth in behavior, subtle and multi-faceted behavior. In art, Pudovkin says, "we term an image realistic if it be a representation of objective reality imaged with maximum exactitude, maximum clarity, maximum profundity, and maximum embrace of its complexity."

In Woodward's behavior as Rachel serving her mother's

friends, in Brando's behavior as Paul at his dead wife's bedside, and in Redgrave's glance at Nancy Neele, we see explored these very elements. Such effective representations of reality call upon the actor's ability to observe in others those small changes in the physiognomy of the face which communicate thought and feeling, and to classify and store these observations for instant recall. The actor must be ready to elicit such responses in himself, to be aware of similar thoughts and feelings in himself, and to know the ways in which they are expressed on his own face. It is essential to understand the differences between his own way of coping and that of others. It is in these differences that the actor can begin to understand and communicate character.

The truth of physical action is easiest to comprehend. Lillian Gish, for instance, in preparing to play a young girl dying of tuberculosis in *Broken Blossoms*, drank no water or liquids for two days and stuffed her mouth with cotton. For such extreme physical characteristics and their effect upon the personality, this is a quick means to understanding. Anne Bancroft rode blindfolded on a roller coaster to prepare herself for the portrayal of Annie Sullivan in *The Miracle Worker*. The impressions she received on the ride would remain with her more vividly than any intellectual analysis of the effects of blindness, because she had experienced it directly in her own body. The actor who considers his body and mind as a computer, and consciously stores away data, will have a greater range of experience to call upon for character than one who is only partially aware of his own psychophysical memory banks.

Understanding of emotional truth is more demanding of the actor's sensitivity. He must be a kind of biofeedback machine. He must be able to empathize with the feelings of others and to note the subtlest changes of feeling revealed in facial expressions and gestures. The actor must intuit the meaning of these slight changes, whether they are designed to hide real feelings or veil other thoughts. Then the actor must be able to recreate these changes of movement using his own face and body. Through exercises he duplicates those stances, expressions, and other body language that he observes. Like Anne Bancroft, he must use his body to imprint those actions into his psychophysical memory. Observation is not enough. It is in the *doing* that the body retains the impression.

Laurence Olivier has said that once he finds the correct nose or eyebrows for a character, he has the *essence* of the person, and the rest of his body and mind can then amalgamate itself into his new image. To give an extreme example, Robert De Niro gained sixty pounds to play the role of the boxer Jake La Motta in *Raging Bull*. The actor lets his own physical being absorb the "other" character. The process might be compared to learning to ride a bicycle. You don't learn to ride by imagining it, you must *do* it. Once you have physically performed the act (or recreated an imagined characteristic), your body retains the knowledge of it.

Life studies, paintings, and images can be starting points for an imaginative entry into characterization. The actor should use any effective means to engage his imagination and begin making emotional connections with the character. Improvising a situation within a room that the character might live in, or using an animal image to physicalize the character's behavior, might add new and interesting elements to the characterization.

The actor might focus on a number of different walks until one seems correct for the character. Or he might investigate the character's pattern of response to others: talking as an inferior, as a superior, or an equal. He might determine the amount of space the character occupies: his way of moving within a room, his ways of sitting, the different ways he holds his body in certain environments—all are decisions the actor must make through *experiencing* them. It is not enough for the actor to imagine them. He must be able to do them, allowing his body to tell him whether they seem correct, almost correct, or totally wrong. Ideally the director will make adjustments in the results of these exercises, using certain elements, changing others, adapting and molding physical details, until they seem organically to express the character. The exercises serve a double function: they sharpen the actor's ability to change his mannerisms and they shed light on the internal and external traits peculiar to the actor.

To prepare himself for the demands of a script, the film actor should habitually catalog data about human behavior. Observing and recreating behavior other than his own stretches his physical and emotional abilities. The more manifestations of thought and feeling the actor can call upon in any given scene, the more selectivity he enjoys in the creation of his role. This applies to both physical and mental characteristics. The actor should always *doubt* his ability to know the right reaction to any action. This doubt forces the actor to explore different responses and seek one that best suits the character. It prevents the actor from leaning too much on his personal style of communication in a role.

Every actor has his own psychophysical behavior, composed of physical actions and mannerisms that express the complexity of his own psychological life. His specific set of behavioral manifestations will perfectly suit only one role. For other roles, the actor must make modifications in his external and internal behavior, and he should be able to make these changes as easily as he might alter the color and style of his hair by putting on a wig. It is essential for the actor to appear perfectly at ease and natural in a new set of psychophysical gestures and behavioral reactions. For the part of Ratso in *Midnight Cowboy*, for example, Dustin Hoffman not only adopted a specific way of walking but changed his voice as well. The nasal, hard-throated manner of speaking he used blended excellently with his other physical manifestations for the character. As Wallace Stanton in *Agatha*, Hoffman used a clipped monotone for his speech pattern. In both films, Hoffman's selection of external behavior was entirely appropriate and natural for the different parts.

The actor must develop a repertoire based on observation of the non-verbal ways that human beings communicate with each other. He must identify the meanings or internal motivations underlying these physical actions and become sensitive to their effects upon others. In the film medium, non-verbal behavior is extremely important. The physical potency of film and the power of the close-up shot heighten the impact of the non-verbal gesture.

How can the actor develop his skill in creating imaginative and organic non-verbal behavior?

- Through improvisations based on the story of the character.
- By recalling past personal experiences which are vivid memories. In this recollection, the actor should not dwell on the feelings aroused but rather on the physical details surrounding the experience—the color of the walls in the room, the degree of light, the pattern of movement in the experience. In every actor's life there are strong patterns of behavior that occur during a crisis. Familiarity with these patterns in his own life will make

the actor more sensitive to observing them in the lives of others.
- Observing animal behavior. Improvisations based on animal behavior may point the way to original or surprising responses and gestures for the actor to use in characterization. The stillness of a preying mantis about to strike, for example, or the circling and moaning of chimpanzees around one of their dead might be translated into interesting human behavior.
- Playing the content of the scene rather than simply the externals.
- Concentrating on the endpoint of the action in a scene rather than on the means of expression.
- Developing a connective stream of thought by paraphrasing dialogue or ideas in between the lines.

The skilled actor looks for a logic beneath the character's actions and imagines a host of physical actions that the character might use to carry out his objectives. What is an objective? The objective is a psychologically motivated physical action of the character. This might also include mental actions in making decisions, judgments, or evaluations. The actor must answer questions about what the characters wants, why he wants it, and how he gets it, before he has a total understanding of the character's objective. The emphasis is on action, not feeling. In reading and re-reading the script, the actor should pay attention to elements such as:

- What the character does.
- What the character says to others, both individually and in groups.
- What actions the character takes during the story.
- What others say about the character to him and to others.

The film actor must be able to express various reactions, exhibiting all the subtle nuances in any one reaction, and to hold that reaction without dissipating its effect for the length of time the director chooses to hold the close-up. In some cases, even the blink of an eye will dissipate the concentrated effect. To be successful the actor must firmly shut out all the mechanical paraphernalia surrounding him during the filming and totally concentrate on his silent response and its subtext.

If an actor is sufficiently objective about his performance, he can learn much from watching the rushes of his daily performances. Is he still completely focused on his thought during the close-ups? Does he sit and stand naturally next to other characters, or has he a tendency to angle his body for the camera, rather than letting the camera focus attention on the actor? Is he competing with the mike to project his voice?

One risk in watching rushes is that the actor may become too self-conscious about his work before the camera. In the midst of creating a character or developing a performance, an actor is especially vulnerable to any comment about his work, no matter whether it arises from his own analysis or that of someone else connected with the film. Sometimes directors, by being too specific in praise of the delivery of a line or a gesture, may inadvertantly clip the actor's wing of confidence and inhibit his naturalness by making him too self-conscious about that particular spot. As a result, the actor may not be able to repeat what the director liked. Both the director and the actor must remember that, at this stage of rehearsal or performance, the actor is delicately balancing his own psyche and that of the character with his own objective appraisal of his work. The actor tries to keep the critic in himself submerged while he does the actual performing. Any comment, especially praise, tilts the balance. The critic wells up to the forefront of consciousness, and then the technician in the actor takes over to attempt to repeat a certain effect. If one can watch the rushes and remain virgin—untouched by the critic or technician within—one can use the objective analysis of his performance.

Examining the rushes to discover what elements of characterization have already been captured on film may help the actor find the rhythms in his role. Rhythm is a basic quality in film, in characterization, and in story. Pieces of film are edited together to recreate the rhythmic flow of life, its conflict and action. The director and editor will select certain shots and angles to precede or follow other shots. The best directors make the best choices—that is, juxtapositions that move the spectator in the direction of the emotion, toward involvement with the story and characters. Normally the actor has no control over this process of selection, and he must depend upon the director's and editor's sense of timing, their intuition about when to cut away from the actor, or how long to hold a pause. The actor depends upon them to protect the relationship of one moment in his performance to the whole of his character. The rushes can give the actor some indication of the direction in which the characterization is going and an understanding of the way in which the director is revealing the character to the audience.

Pudovkin in his *Film Acting* was very adamant that actors be allowed to assist in the editing of a film. In essense the actor, the director, and the editor are collaborating on a piece of music, and like a musical composition, with its recurring themes, subthemes, and counterpoints, a film must emphasize, with precision and exactitude, each part in relationship to the others. Certainly a sensitive actor would be an asset in determining the relationship of one shot to another and the effect of the movement from one shot to another. Perhaps the actor's participation is not often encouraged or allowed because our film actors usually do not know enough about the aesthetics of editing. Often they may not be interested in taking on this responsibility or may not be considered qualified by directors and editors.

The rushes can also be valuable to the actor in determining the condition and effect of such important elements as his costume and makeup. Of course, the actor will have worked out his makeup in advance of the shooting with the makeup artists, especially if there are aging changes or a need to resemble a famous personality. Since Ingmar Bergman believes that creativity in film begins with the human face, he always uses his camera movement to give the greatest possible emphasis and strength to the actor's expression. Whatever makeup the actor uses, it is important that it reflect the personality he is trying to develop for the camera. Moreover, it is essential that what the actor expresses and the manner of expressing it conform to the needs of the character as well as the needs of the camera.

THE ZEN OF ACTING

To the Japanese, art is the form-language of the human soul. Acting is the form-language of the human soul in action. Many of the essential characteristics the Zen find in Japanese art can also be used as a basis for the actor and his role. Marvin Zeman in an article in *The Film Journal* lists seven characteristics of Zen art: asymmetry, simplicity, agedness, naturalness, latency, unconventionality, and quietness. The actor uses images to stimulate his imagination in selecting the details used in his characterization, and these Zen qualities are helpful both in beginning the imaginative process of creating a character, and in assuring that the characterization is multi-faceted.

Asymmetry—an imbalance or disharmony of proportions—should lead the actor to discover first of all how the character is tainted. No character consists of only one trait. The portrayal of the saint should include his unsaintly qualities. The shining knight should have a chink in his armor. In every role it is more interesting for the actor and for the spectator to see the opposite side of the character's main trait. Even when he is using his own personality to play the character, he should be open to his own failings, to those traits which make it difficult to keep up the image he plays for the

Simplicity in film acting is the omission of all insignificant or irrelevant details. It covers the scaling down of the size and magnitude of acting for the camera to a more intimate and naturalistic method, as well as selecting only those physical characteristics and mental or emotional orientations which are essential. Even a personality actor must be aware that he can become a caricature of himself if he does not pick and choose among his own personal mannerisms for each role.

The Zen quality of agedness communicates itself in art as a calm outlook on life. In acting, every actor must seem to be at ease in the environment in which he finds himself, and in the personality that the writer or filmmaker has developed. He must relate to the action naturally. The ease which results when the actor does respond organically to the stimuli of environment, conflict, and action, engenders an ease in the spectator.

Naturalness is basic to the art of film acting. At no time must we see any tension of the actor underneath the character. At no time must we be aware of the compulsion of the actor to indicate things rather than seemingly experience them. Any forcing of emotion will be obvious, and any "commenting" on the theme or comedy will be read along with the actions of the character. In film you must look into the eyes of the other actor and relate to *him*, not

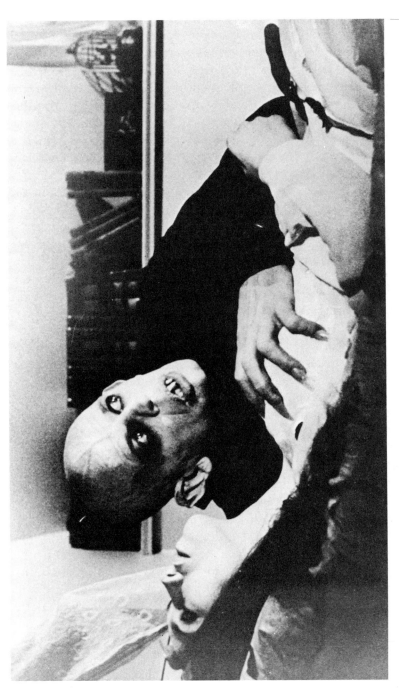

Isabelle Adjani and Klaus Kinski in Werner Herzog's Nosferatu.

to some idea you have of the character he is playing. Watch him closely for any signs that he is being affected by your actions. Try to take him by surprise, and let his reaction affect you.

Latency in art reveals the "infinite heaven in a puddle." Like Glenda Jackson's finger-in-the-mouth gesture during the death scene of *Elizabeth R*, or Brando's upside-down greeting from his horse in *The Missouri Breaks*, gestures should say more than the obvious physical action required. The gesture should communicate what the character needs, or what the character unconsciously wants to communicate. The actor must learn to cover the character's needs whenever possible, to hide the real feelings. He should find ways to fail in the coverup, to let the hidden needs and desires momentarily surface.

Instead of trying to devise a pattern of behavior based on cause and effect, the film actor should be open to those unconventional, odd moments of behavior, those vulnerable responses which the actor himself makes without preparation. Even making mistakes can be a blessing. As sculptor Isamu Noguchi states, "The accident can give you the key to creation."

In every art, quietness is harmony. In film acting, harmony of the external form, internal needs, vocal expression, physical gesture, relationship to the environment, costume, makeup, and duality of purpose develop a performance that is consistent, holistic, and imaginative.

It is a special privilege to be able to use one's body, voice, emotional memory, and mental capability to interpret and construct the human characteristics of an imaginary being. It requires concentration, relaxation, observation, physical and vocal control, plus a desire to become another person for a short period of time. Images of the human condition are preserved for us on film. The actor can study the methods of developing character on film from the Delsartian stylized gestures of the early silent films to the realism of modern *cinéma vérité*. He will find ways to relate to the proper psychological circumstances to evoke subtle gesture and spontaneous response. He will forget that he is surrounded by machinery and seek to reproduce the essence of reality for the camera with restraint and relaxation. He will lend his past experiences, his intuitions, his mind and body to develop and refine the film actor's art: the art of revealing what Shakespeare called "the mind's construction on the face."

Donald Sutherland in Roeg's Don't Look Now.

III
Deep Focus

10

ANALYSIS OF A FILM PERFORMANCE

To better understand the art and craft of the film actor, let us make a detailed examination of a movie remarkable for the quality of acting: Brian De Palma's *Carrie*, with Sissy Spacek.

Carrie is the story of an insecure teenager whose sexual and psychic anxiety result in telekinesis, the ability to move objects. Debased by her high school peers, who shower her with a bucket of pig's blood during her crowning as Prom Queen, Carrie maniacally destroys the entire gymnasium and its occupants, then leaves to kill her mother and herself. This horror tale is expertly directed by De Palma and graphically acted by Sissy Spacek.

A close analysis of the film and its various shots enables us to break down the actor's work into separate aspects: acting, action, and geography. The *acting* as we categorize it in this analysis consists of those scenes which require the actor to share dialogue with other characters in the pursuit of some objective, and to react to the other characters and to events. *Action* refers to those scenes in which the actor does things, movements which do not in themselves create any progression of emotion. *Geography* refers to those scenes in which the actor's presence helps to locate the film in a specific place and time, setting the atmosphere and mood as well as the geography.

A beginning actor reading a script for the first time will do well to note the percentage of acting scenes for his character within the script. The more there are, the easier it will be to establish character, and the more challenging it will be for the actor to create character. *Carrie* is an excellent choice for this kind of analysis because it contains so many acting scenes. The shot analysis is limited to the particular character of Carrie. We begin with the geography.

There are eight places in which the character's action occurs:

> Carrie's home—her room upstairs, and the downstairs areas (the closet and bathroom).
> A high school yard.
> The locker room and showers.
> A classroom.
> The library.
> A drugstore.
> The gymnasium.
> A car.

Those shots which serve mainly to establish location or geography are the following:

> Walking down a sidewalk to her home.
> Waiting outside the principal's office.
> Sitting in the classroom.
> Sitting on the stairs in her home.
> Looking into the gym through a window.
> Walking into the drugstore.
> Walking into the decorated gymnasium.

The action or activity shots include:

> Playing volleyball.
> Taking a shower.
> Crouching in the closet.
> Picking out and reading books on telekinesis.
> Pinning her dress on a dress model.
> Trying on makeup.
> Sitting in the car before going into the Prom.
> Crossing to the stage to be crowned.
> Dancing with Tommy.
> Being showered with the pig's blood.
> Crossing to the gym exit.
> Walking down the road away from the school.

Arriving home.

Crossing through rooms to the bathroom at home.

Taking a bath.

Dressing after the bath.

In the movie there are many challenging acting scenes:

Carrie's reaction to missing the volleyball.

Reaction to having her first menstruation: she runs through the locker room, clutching at the others, begging for help.

The geography of the room is set by the opening shots of the group of girls dressing, chatting, and roughhousing.

Scene with Miss Collins, who comforts Carrie.

Scene with the Principal. He calls her by an incorrect name. After correcting his mistake several times she focuses her anger on the ashtray which is tossed from the desk by her power.

Scene with her mother about the school incident. Carrie has overheard her mother's responses to the telephone call from the school official. Carrie asks her mother why she never told her about menstruation. The mother, vividly played by Piper Laurie, forces Carrie into the closet.

Carrie's reaction inside the closet. She lights a candle under the crucifix.

Reaction in class to the poem written by Tommy.

Scene with Tommy in the library in which he asks her to go to the prom.

Scene with Miss Collins in which she tries to convince Carrie that she's beautiful.

Scene with Tommy at the screen door of her home. He again asks her to go to the prom. She doesn't want her mother to hear the conversation.

Scene with her mother about going to the prom. Carrie tells her mother things are going to be different. Several objects are hurled through the air as a threat.

Scene with her mother while Carrie is applying her last-minute makeup before Tommy arrives.

Scene with Tommy in the car outside gym. Carrie is hesitant about going in, reluctant to face the other students.

> Scenes with Tommy at the table in the gym.
> Scene with Miss Collins at the table in the gym. Carrie tells
> Miss Collins how happy she is.
> Scene with Tommy about voting for the King and Queen of
> the Prom.
> Carrie's reaction to the shower of pig's blood
> Carrie's harnessing her telekinetic power and using it to
> destroy the gym.
> Scene with mother upstairs after taking a bath. Mother
> cradles Carrie in her arms, and then stabs her. Carrie
> gets up, and in the struggle falls down the stairs.
> Scene with her mother downstairs in their home. Through
> telekinesis Carrie pins the mother to the doorjambs and
> kills her.
> Scene dragging her mother into the closet.

Each of these acting scenes is composed of many shots, some lasting as little as two or three seconds, all relating to character action and reaction. Sissy Spacek as Carrie appears in approximately forty minutes of the film. In that time she creates one of the most memorable characters in a horror film. It is important to recall that each shot in the final print represents a miniscule portion of what was actually rehearsed and shot during the filming.

Spacek's characterization is based on a selection of physical qualities, mannerisms, and reactions that vividly convey the personality of Carrie, her fears, and her hopes.

The role is built upon these physicalizations:

> Crouching.
> Clutching at people.
> Unkempt, straggling hair.
> Holding books to her chest in a self-protective manner.
> Huddled positions in which she seems to enfold herself.
> Stiff-kneed walk.
> Hair-consciousness. She toys with and twists her hair, she
> straightens her hair, she runs her hands through her hair,
> particularly in the seconds before she moves objects.
> Eye glances to make sure no one's watching her awkward
> body. She often holds her arms tightly behind her back.
> Little use of direct eye contact in the scenes before the prom
> bid.

Sissy Spacek and Piper Laurie during the final scene in Carrie.

Her physical demeanor gradually changes at the prom:

> She enters clutching her shawl.
> Slowly smiles at others.
> Laughs in a relaxed and easy way.
> Embraces others.
> Occasionally still holds on to herself, using a protective gesture like clutching her right shoulder with her left hand.
> Pulls hands rapidly off the table and covers her eyes with both hands when Tommy suggests they vote for themselves.
> Toys with her hair when she and Tommy are declared the winners.
> Broad smiles, and restrained tears combined with an awed expression when she is crowned.

After the initial shock, the gruesome shower of pig's blood provokes an entirely new set of mannerisms:

> Opens mouth in a silent scream.
> Hands move quickly up to her head.
> Her body stiffens.
> Her eyes are wide open and staring.
> Her walk is stiff, the arms and hands held away from her body.

As Carrie arrives back at her home following the destruction of the gym, her physical identity is reminiscent of a robot:

> Her head and neck are thrust forward and held stiffly in that position as she walks.
> Her arms are still held rigidly away from her body, one hand poised in a stiffly bent position.

In the death scene, Carrie reverts back to the huddled and crouched body mannerism:

> Crouches huddled in a corner, her hands clutching at the doorknob as her mother approaches her with the knife.
> Listens, but turns only her eyes in the direction of her dying mother.
> Cradles the mother as fire consumes the house.

From this analysis list of the shots, we can cull the basic gestures and mannerisms which compose the signature of Carrie's character. Opposing the clutching, nervous hair tugging and downcast eye movements are two other character traits: the towering rage, and the blossoming of a young woman in a moment of fulfillment with twinkling eyes, broad smiles, and an other-worldly joy that pervades her face. These choices are not acciden-tal. The character is a well-conceived execution based on intelligent selection of physical traits and mannerisms.

Within this overall characterization, there are individual mo-ments of inventive action which should be noted. The childlike and childish actions Carrie performs form a basis for the tremendous anxiety that controls her life. They also serve to make credible the cruelest temper tantrum in film. The actions which project the child in Carrie include her kicking at the wall as her mother drags her to the closet, folding her hands in prayer, toying with her hair before kissing her mother after the closet punishment is over. She places her thumb on her mouth when Tommy talks to her in the library, pulls her sweater sleeves over her hands in her conversation with Miss Collins about whether or not she is pretty.

The numerous physical references to her hair and head form the physical connection to her psychic anxiety and telekinetic powers. Before almost every telekinetic experience, Carrie places her hands on the sides of her head, or runs her hands through her hair. The hair-tugging, -twisting, and -toying occur during mo-ments of contradiction and stress, when the character finds it difficult to assert herself in a natural, outgoing manner.

The clothing Carrie wears also helps to identify her shy, childlike attributes and the emerging young woman. One of her first outfits is an old-fashioned sailor-collared blouse and skirt, reminiscent of the uniform dress for young women in the early part of the century. Tie oxfords and white knee socks complete the drab look. It sets her apart from the other young women in the film. The dress she makes for the prom, however, is a pink slip-like gown that is both innocent and nubile, reminiscent of Harlow's gowns in films of the thirties.

In terms of characterization, this is a well-designed develop-ment of personality in which both the actor and the director used discretion in the selection and execution of physical mannerisms and emotional reactions. Spacek's and De Palma's Carrie is a thoughtful characterization, whose design provokes engagement of the audience.

IV
Practical Matters

11

THE INTERVIEW
AND AUDITION

You are being considered for a role in a film. What happens next? Probably the first contact you have will be with the director at an interview. Jon Voight refers to this occasion as "taking a meeting." The interview might be held in an office or during lunch at a restaurant. Other people might be included in this meeting—actors, producers, or writers. It will appear to be a social event, but everyone involved knows important decisions are in the process of being made.

The director's uppermost thoughts will be whether or not your personality traits are right for the part. Moviemaking is an expensive business. Time can't be wasted trying to transform an ingenue into a character actor or leading lady. It is crucial to be yourself at this meeting. The camera will project all you have to offer, and the director will be making judgment after judgment about your traits, your physical presence, and your willingness to adapt to various suggestions.

Remember that physical features are important, so you should wear what you feel most comfortable in. If you can handle the transformation naturally, wear what you think the character might wear. There are many examples of actors who changed their images by selecting and wearing the right clothing to suit the character. Shelley Winters attributes being cast in *A Place in the Sun* to her wearing a coat belonging to her sister. The coat seemed to Winters to be just the right style for the character. Wearing it, Winters could appear less the "glamor girl" she was considered at the time. Michelle Phillips in her lunch interview with Ken Russell for a role in *Valentino* dressed in a quasi-1920s style, a headband across her forehead. Marlon Brando requested a screen test be done for his consideration as the Godfather in the movie of the same name. For the test, he purchased the clothing, and added tissues to his mouth, puffing up his lower jaw. The effect was astonishing, and kept in during the filming of the movie.

At this first interview with the director and others, a particular role may or may not be discussed. The director may be considering you for one of several parts in the film. It is difficult to pinpoint exactly what the director is looking for in you. You may be certain, though, that no director wants to work with an actor who is difficult, unless, of course, that actor is enormously "bankable." This means that the actor's name will carry enough weight for banks to put up the money for the film. In this case, the "name" is probably interviewing the director.

The close working conditions in film require that all the artists be able to get along together. It isn't necessary to be ultra chummy, but it is helpful if the director sees you as a person who will contribute, not one who will question or balk at his every suggestion or decision.

If a specific role is discussed, you should certainly give your impression of the character based on your knowledge of the script. You may have personal or work experiences that relate to the character's. Mention these in your discussion of the character. If you are willing to change your appearance, let the director know. Federico Fellini likes his lead actors to lose weight before a film, not only because the weight loss makes it easier to light and film them, but also because he believes that becoming thinner also gives the actor a look of being "ravaged inside." Robert De Niro gained sixty pounds in order to play his conception of the fighter in *Raging Bull*. Shelley Winters gained nearly as much for her role in *The Poseidon Adventure*.

In preparation for a career in film acting, it is important for the actor to keep body weight at a good level, to follow a program of regular exercise to keep the body flexible and to build stamina. These physical qualities will be noted by the director at the first interview. He may not comment on them, but he will note them.

Use your eyes in communicating during the interview. Make direct contact with anyone you're speaking to. Straightforward communication is important to credibility in film. Compare the film personalities of such actors as Goldie Hawn, Madeline Kahn, and Marsha Mason. All are high-spirited and gifted in comedy. All have infectious grins and laughs. All seem to be avid listeners. One can imagine a director becoming immediately engaged by these personalities.

Contrast these three women with three male actors: Al Pacino, Robert De Niro, and Michael Moriarity. All appear to have intense, thoughtful personalities. Each conveys a slightly sullen aspect to his character, not an unlikeable aspect, but one which provokes curiosity and interest. If a director wished to cast three women of the *same aspects* opposite these three men, he would not be looking for a Hawn, Kahn, or Mason. More likely he would be looking for someone like Meryl Streep, Jessica Lange, or Teresa Russell. Male actors analogous in type to Hawn, Kahn, or Mason would be James Caan, George Segal, or Chevy Chase. These examples are obvious ones, and in no way meant to infer limits on the kind of roles any of these actors *could* play. We use them in these groupings to illustrate the potency of personality, whether it be on screen or off.

At your interview, be yourself. Have confidence in the fact that your personality is unique. You needn't try to imitate anyone. You may be similar in type to another actor but your idiosyncratic attributes are unique to you. Be at ease with yourself. Don't try too hard to please or to call undue attention to your particular talents. The director may be missing those, but seeing much different ones.

Try not to confuse rejection of your type for rejection of your self. The movies are a business. If the producers or directors want cornflakes, they won't accept caviar. Their decisions are no reflection on you as a person. They indicate only that your attributes are not the commodities they are looking for *at this time*. The more an actor remains convinced of the separation between his talent and the way it is packaged and his ego, the easier it is for him to continue looking for work in the film business. Charlton Heston refers to these groups of actors interviewing and auditioning for work as the "brave parade." Indeed, you must be brave to continue putting yourself through interviews and auditions when the outcome is so risky.

This self-confidence or serenity of self is a quality that every actor must continue to have, no matter how successful he becomes. There is always the possibility that he will not be marketable during some stage in his career. Aging will alter his access to all roles. Adjustments must be made continually during any actor's career. It is easier if a beginning actor develops this serenity early on in his career.

Even though a director may well decide during an interview you are not "quite right" for this particular role, he may notice some unique attribute that he could use in the future. Many actors have not been cast the first time around, yet have been remembered and cast by directors at work on entirely new projects months or years later.

Not all interviews are conducted in such regulated or formal ways. Some directors will arrange for a casual, social group encounter for their first look at actors. For one of his films, Steven Spielberg arranged a meeting with actors in a home where they all were invited into the kitchen to make cookies or some other goodies. Occasionally, during the informal get-together, some Spielberg associate would shoot some film of the actors. This seems a very good way to test actors. They are engaged in some activity which has a very specific goal (i.e., good-tasting cookies) and they are apt to be more natural in this circumstance.

After the first interview the director may ask you to read a scene for him on camera. In this event, you will be given a short scene to read and perhaps memorize. A video camera may be used to shoot this reading. Photographs will certainly be taken at some point during the audition. You may or may not have a partner in the scene—the other roles may not yet be cast, or the budget may not allow bringing in one or more actors to do the scene with you. This screen or camera test may last as long as two to three hours, depending upon the director's method. Karen Allen, cast as Marion Ravenwood in *Raiders of the Lost Ark*, was given the scene in which Marion first meets Indiana Jones. She did this scene with two or three different actors, each session lasting two or more hours, before she was finally cast. At such auditions, the director may ask you to try several different ways of playing the scene; he may give you several different images for the character and ask you to try them out as you read the lines.

You should try to be as open to suggestion as you possibly can during such an audition. This can be a learning and developing experience for the actor, as well as an audition or screen test. Don't be afraid to "dive in" and try these new things. An adventuresome spirit is an asset in moviemaking and film acting. Try to use some physical trait for the character. Some physicalization of the internal life adds dimension to your audition and also gives the actor something to focus on during this tense time. Make some decisions about the character after you have read the scene. Decide on the character's relationship to the others. Decide to play one specific objective during the scene. If another actor is available to you in the audition, use him. Make contact with him, move him, let him affect you. You will be letting the director know you are serious about your work as an actor, are able to play with the ensemble, and are willing to make adjustments.

Whether or not you are cast by the director, you should write him a note of thanks or appreciation. As time passes, and you have other roles, you might let any director you have auditioned for know what you have been doing since his audition. Keep up the contacts you have made. Directors must have actors, just as actors must have roles, to do their jobs.

Although auditioning is never easy, it is a skill that can be learned and developed. Many theatres and universities are now offering workshops in auditioning. The film actor should take advantage of these courses and polish his interview and audition skills. Other actors in the courses will share their experiences with you, and their fears and hopes, too. The audition is a necessary evil, but the actor can make it a pleasant experience by regarding it as an opportunity to reveal his talent.

12

SPECIAL EFFECTS

Acting in a film using special effects requires several specialized techniques. A film may use either mechanical or optical special effects, both of which produce certain acting problems. Mechanical special effects have a direct bearing upon the actor since he must adjust to and incorporate them in his action and reactions on the set. Optical special effects are produced in a laboratory and added on later to the print of the film. Optical special effects affect the actor in the sense that there is something missing from his setting: mechanical special effects add another dimension to the set.

In *Raiders of the Lost Ark*, for example, Harrison Ford as Indiana Jones had to dodge mechanical arrows in one of the early scenes in the film. In *Superman*, Margot Kidder (Lois Lane) and Christopher Reeve (Superman) fly around the world. In the studio Kidder and Reeve were both mechanically harnessed separately and together in their flight positions. The scene is acted before a blue screen on which will be added the optical geographical shots of their journey. Many of Alec Guinness's scenes as Obi Wan Kenobi in *Star Wars* were shot in front of a blue screen or moving mattes, both of which are used for optical effects.

Mechanical special effects include such contraptions as harness rigs, blood bags, squibs, rain, snow, and sand storms. A harness is a mechanical support worn by the actor to keep him in a position which he could not normally sustain himself. Everyone is familiar with the harness and flying rig used for the numerous stage productions of *Peter Pan*. A similar rig was used for Kidder and Reeve in *Superman*. The two actors were harnessed together for long periods of time during the many takes of their flying scenes. These mechanical devices demand extraordinary patience and stamina on the part of the actors involved. It is strenuous work to maintain a believable attitude when you're wearing a harness exerting a tremendous amount of physical strain on your body.

Plaster casts are often made of actors' faces, hands, and other parts of the body. The molds are later used to create masks or body parts for special effect scenes, such as the death of Belloq in *Raiders of the Lost Ark*. Sitting for a plaster cast of the face is a grueling experience. The actor's face is first vaselined. Dentist's plaster or a similar substance is applied to the face. The drying process takes approximately thirty to forty minutes, during which time the actor can breathe only through the two straws inserted into his nostrils. Needless to say, the actor must remain still, or as still as possible, during the process in order to obtain a usable mold. Claustrophobia and an overwhelming feeling of sensory deprivation often set in after the first five minutes. Imagine the experience of actor Anthony Daniels, who had to wait while a plaster cast was made of his entire body to serve as a model for his "suit" as C-3PO. A latex suit over an undersuit fitted with cold water circulation tubes was used in the final design. Being totally encased in this robot suit demanded great adjustments from Daniels both as person and actor. Personal demands include patience, stamina, and resilience. As an actor, Daniels had to incorporate a certain amount of mime into his characterization.

Actors who are involved in violent scenes requiring a bloody wound are equipped with squibs. A squib is a small remote-controlled explosive device. For a "blood hit" a squib is attached to a plate worn next to the skin under the clothing. A "blood" bag is taped to the squib. Wires controlling the small explosion are run from the plate down the leg. At the proper cue, a remote control triggers the charge which bursts the blood bag and the clothing material, creating the illusion of a bloody injury. No matter how skilled the actor is at stunts, the moment of the explosion is always a tense one. He must trust his safety to the special-effects technicians, most of whom are highly qualified in a discipline demanding rigid safety conditions.

Squibs made of soft bricks covered with plasticine can also be used for explosions in battle settings around the actor. These are implanted in the set at various points and are triggered on cues worked out in expert detail by the technicians. Stunt persons are used for these highly dangerous ground explosions, if the character must appear visually hit. The director will use the actor to get as close as possible to the actual explosion time, cut the action, and then substitute the stunt person. Even in these stunt double cases, there is always a safety line beyond which no person is allowed.

Special effects of any kind are usually sketched out and gone over from cue to cue by the special-effects coordinator before each scene. Actors are told exactly what is going to happen, when it will occur, and where they should remain on the selected cues. It is up to the individual actor to use good sense and precaution in any special effects scene.

Some mechanical special effects require expert timing on the actor's part. In *Raiders of the Lost Ark*, Harrison Ford as Indiana Jones must dodge innumerable darts from holes in the walls of the South American temple he explores. If these tiny arrows had been optically produced, all Ford would have had to do was run through the space, dodging at will, creating his own sense of arrows whizzing through the space around him. Optical effects would have set the arrows in motion to coordinate with his movements, artificially creating a "near-miss" effect. The arrows, however, were mechanically produced, and Ford actually had to dodge them as they whizzed out from the holes. This places the burden of timing and coordination on the actor as well as the technicians, but it also produces a more realistic scene.

Electrical rigs are sometimes set inside a piece of furniture or prop dressing the set. In *Raiders of the Lost Ark*, for instance, electricals were placed inside the mummies in the catacombs so arms could appear to be moving. Actual movement of a prop on the floor while shooting is an aid to the actor because it supports his ability to react believably. Once again, the actor will be given a warning cue, either verbal or physical, to prepare for the prop to move. The repetition of takes may strain the actor's credibility. It is easy to react believably the first few times, when you are genuinely surprised by the sudden movement. It is much harder to do it effortlessly on the twentieth take. The actor's tendency is to structure his reaction too much on the later takes, making it appear overly studied. One method some actors use to keep spontaneity is to distract themselves in some minute, specific way several seconds before the cue, or concentrate on the moments and the goal beyond the special effects cue.

Other mechanical effects challenge the actor's projection of credibility. In order for rain and sand storms to be picked up by the camera, the rain and sand have to be at least twice as much as one would think necessary for the effect. The actor in a light rain or sand storm is actually being pelted fairly heavily by the substance. Smoke is usually created by setting tires afire. Imagine the odor of burning rubber which assaults the actor's sense of smell. In a movie such as *Apocalypse Now*, the actor must play such a scene without reacting to this odor, but rather reacting to the struggles of war.

High falls ending with a visible impact between the actor and the ground are usually executed in collaboration between the actor and the stunt double. The fall area is covered with safety pads, or rigs, at least eight feet wide and twelve feet long. These rigs are made of cardboard boxes, sponge rubber sheets, or sponge blocks packed in a bag. Air bags are also used as fall rigs by some technicians. The stunt double will execute a fall from whatever height the scene demands. In most cases, the height of the fall is no more than fifty feet. The director will shoot the fall, then get another shot in which the actor falls from a distance under five feet. These two shots are cut together so that approximately 75 percent of the fall is the footage of the stunt double's fall, and the remainder is footage of the actor's five-foot fall.

To execute a fall from any distance demands muscular coordination, timing, and stamina. The actor would benefit by enlisting the aid of the stunt technicians, and stunt doubles to teach him the rudiments of stunt activity. There are many methods of preparing the body for stunts, executing stunts, and recovering from stunts that can be shared by the technicians. Acting in a movie using numerous special effects is a job promising bruises, bumps, and some battering of the body, no matter how much of the heavy stunt work is executed by professionals. For *Star Wars*, Mark Hamill did fourteen takes of bumping his head on a precise mark!

Breakaway furniture, walls, or other set pieces, such as the statue in *Raiders of the Lost Ark*, present several kinds of difficulties to the actor. Breakaway furniture and walls are rigged so that they must be used in a specific way in order to break. Very often the actor misses the mark, or the technician misses the connection, and nothing happens. Pound on the piece as he may, it stands firm. An inch or two to the left or right, and a gentle touch will cause it to fall apart. *The Carol Burnett Show* very often used outtakes of actors trying to make breakaway furniture "break" as comic bits. In the heat of a scene, the actor has to concentrate not only on the action of the moment, but also must keep one part of his brain concentrated on where the final punch must hit. The coordination must be exact in order to make things work. The right and left sides of the brain must be working together, no easy task in any job, but crucial to the actor's art.

For the statue fall in *Raiders of the Lost Ark*, Ford had to be on the statue right before it fell. The director shot his reactions up to the actual moment, which indicates that Ford had to act *as if* the statue were beginning to crumble. This is a particularly good example of Stanislavsky's dictum that the actor must respond *as if* he were in the particular set of circumstances given by the author. For the actual fall of the statue, a stunt double was used to take Ford's place. The statue was equipped with special handholds and safety pads to protect double Martin Grace during the fall.

Raiders of the Lost Ark provided another kind of special-effects experience for the actors: the use of live and dangerous reptiles. Thousands of reptiles were involved in the "Well of the Souls" shot. These included cobras, boa constrictors, pythons, and grass snakes. Snake serum was on hand for any injuries from snake bites, of course. Imagine being asked to stand among these dangerous reptiles for long periods of time for separate takes of shots required for the scene. In these kinds of circumstances, the actor needs a healthy dose of intestinal fortitude. Stunt doubles or snake handlers could be used for some of the shots, but the principal actors had to be seen among the snakes for certain shots to work. Is the fear on the actors' faces acting? The almost universal fear and queasiness that most people feel regarding snakes would contribute 90 percent of the actors' reactions. The "as if" method in this set of circumstances doesn't apply; the actors are in the circumstances. An actor needn't worry about playing a reaction—he will respond to such an environment.

Werner Herzog's *Nosferatu* had a similar scene in which hundreds of rats scurried around townspeople at a dining table set in the square. Like the snakes in *Raiders of the Lost Ark*, the rats in *Nosferatu* needed constant control by set technicians. Corralling and herding these mini-beasts to the setup area was a continuous effort.

The actors' job was to stay in the camera range; the technicians' job was to stay out of camera range while keeping the rats and snakes in the shots.

How do actors learn to do falls, stand among rats, or use a breakaway prop? Stunt experts on the set can teach the actor the techniques, the practical skills, and safety procedures. It is up to the actor to practice the techniques so that he can execute various special actions properly. In the moments of shooting on the floor, the actor has one final guardian for his safety—himself. As for grisly chores, such as standing amid snakes or rats, the actor has to make a decision whether or not he can do this kind of job in a film. Some actors won't do nude scenes; others won't act with dangerous animals. Once an actor has committed himself to a job, it is his responsibility to execute it as well as he can. In the weeks or months between signing the contract and shooting the film, the actor can learn many skills. Many actors must learn simple skills like riding a horse, swimming, or diving from a board. In a recent film with Katharine Hepburn, Jane Fonda had to execute a back flip off a diving board. She had never done it before, but was determined to add this skill to her techniques. This willingness and adaptability are important elements in film acting.

Optical special effects create a different problem for the actor. An actor's work is usually closely involved with reality. He works in specific locations, allowing the geography of the place to influence his camera behavior. He works with specific, real props on location or on a set. These real settings, furniture, and props help the actor to believe in what he is doing. With the use of optical special effects, something very important is missing from the setting.

The early use of optical special effects was very crude because it was obvious. Actors in a mock-up car, for instance, were placed in front of a screen on which would be projected moving highway traffic or scenery passing by. The actor was without a very important partner in his work—the real location or setting. Today, optical special effects are so technologically advanced that very often we are unaware of their use in a movie. In a single shot we may actually be seeing four shots layered one by one over the base print. At the time of shooting the actor does not have a specific relationship to everything in the shot, since many things will be

Production crew herding the rats for a scene in Nosferatu.

added in the lab. In these cases, the actor's imagination has to be totally engaged. He must imagine he is seeing great sights from a great distance in the sky, as Margot Kidder did in *Superman*. Specificity is the key to playing these kinds of scenes. The actor must select specific objects that he visualizes in his imagination. Glances must be held in one direction for certain lengths of time, dictated by the director. Quick changes in eye direction would not work in these situations. The actor has to take into account the geography and the climate of the setting to be added and respond accordingly. In *Superman*, fans blowing on the actors undoubtedly helped to produce the effect of flying. The awe and splendor of the flight in Kidder's eyes came from her imagination.

Play is an essential element in the actor's relationship to missing special effects. The childlike sense of play which enables the actor to believe he is where the director says he is, to react to his idea of the place—this sense of play or pretending is the root of good acting. Like all roots, it has to be properly nourished. In acting, the root is play; the soil is experience and observation.

13

EXERCISES

These exercises are designed to expand the actor's awareness of his physical, mental, and emotional resources, and to develop the ability to adapt a variety of physical traits and behaviors. Do the exercises for a video camera, if possible, and analyze the results.

Tribal Persona

Select any piece of music. As you listen to the music, pick up several objects within your range and create a sculpture, a sign, or something with no specific meaning. Follow your instinctual and intuitive response to the music. When you have finished, step back and respond to your placement of the found objects.

Life Study

Spend fifteen or twenty minutes observing another person in the midst of an *actively* physical task or sport. Without making judgments on the personality of the observed person, recreate in exact detail the physical mannerisms and body language.

Imitation

In a silent sequence of activity, imitate a relative or close friend in the midst of any activity you have observed. Add the spoken word after you have finished the silent sequence.

Body Language

Write a brief and specific description of your body language. Exchange descriptions with another person. Execute the body language you read. While the other person is recreating your body language, analyze what personality traits are being projected through the physical.

Silent Action

Devise a silent activity to music for two minutes. You must stretch or complete the action so that it fills the musical space.

Example: You enter camera range. A table holds stacks of plates, glasses, silverware, napkins, etc. Set the table within the time limit of the music. Your objective is to set the table correctly. Make several adjustments to the objective: you have never set a table before; you have recently received bad news; you are anxious to finish the task and do something else.

Sneak Attack

Use dialogue from a scene between two people. Both actors are seated, drinking coffee. Actor A has poison pellets concealed on his person. He must drop the pellets into the drink of Actor B during the dialogue.

Listening

Listen on cue to a sound which surprises, annoys, or frightens you. Look right or left in the direction of the sound. Analyze the videotape. Was the reaction overdone? Does the head turn too quickly? Too slowly? Repeat and refine.

Props

Select three props which you think will characterize a person.

Invent a short sequence using the props. Repeat the sequence of activity three times, each time using the props in a different way, to characterize personality.

Reactions

On camera, *overact* the following: seeing someone you love enter your view; seeing someone you dislike enter your view; seeing someone who owes you money enter your view.

Repeat the three reactions with as little facial movement as possible. Repeat the three reactions with no facial expression. What you now consider no facial expression may contain some kind and degree of response.

The Other

Select articles of clothing from a costume room, and build a character around them. Wear the clothing which inspires you. On camera, answer questions in a natural way about this "other" person. Where were you born? How many in your family, etc.? Analyze the "other's" behavior. What facial and bodily mannerisms emerged in the character? What is the personal orientation to life of your character?

Props II

Drink or eat something while carrying on a memorized dialogue or monologue on camera. Use the food or drink to avoid carrying on the conversation. Then eat or drink because you haven't had any nourishment for a long time. Continue to carry on the speaking and relating to other characters during the eating and drinking.

V
Actors and Directors on Film Acting

14

INTERVIEWS WITH PROFESSIONALS AT WORK

The following are excerpts from comments by professional actors and directors now working in America and in England. Some were interviewed personally by the author; others responded to a written questionnaire.

NICOLAS ROEG

Director: *Walkabout, Performance, Don't Look Now, Bad Timing*

O'BRIEN: *When you start work on a film, what kind of relationships do you establish with the actors, and the work ahead? What is your method of working?*

ROEG: I never think of casting at all. I never even think of what the people look like in the story until they're captured. Even as the characters are being written, I think of them as changing shapes and sizes. I don't like to get a picture of the person in my mind—this character is a dark, sallow, swarthy man—and then get locked into that. With the place too, I can't really get a picture of the places. It's just a gray image of the place, really, and what the things are in that place . . . I'm trying to analyze how I work. As for the people—

I never think this part would be wonderful for so and so; she's exactly the right person . . . especially if you don't know the person, if you've just seen them as a star, or an actor. That sort of casting is being pressed far more and more in the cinema. But it wouldn't work.

Once the script is finished, I feel it's got to be shot now. The script, too, comes in stages. It's not *quite* finished. I don't *quite* put the finishing touches on it and say, "That's it!" Then go to someone and say "Here's the script. Would you like to do it" and never change it. I think that's another difference between film and the theatre. The playwright turns over his script.

So many of the elements as I work are gray images. Sooner or later it gets to the point where I think, "That's as far as I can go." Then it needs to be shot.

And then I like to stand back and think, "I wonder who these people are . . . who are they?" And you start trying to keep as open a mind as you can. It sounds quite random. You start thinking about the type of person a character is; what his background is. And then you think of all the actors and performers there are who might play this person. Not just actors and performers, though. I was thinking not long ago of a rich, young man in New York I know, as a possibility for a film. I'd just like to coax him into being himself on film.

O'BRIEN: *Your observation of people in life, whether or not you're working on a film, seems an acute one.*

ROEG: Maybe. But not self-consciously. I see people who could be used in film. I think people come to things. If they've got that kind of openness to it. Once you start directing something, it's rather like a horse in a race. You just guide it, encourage the horse to go. It's got to have its head.

O'BRIEN: *Donald Sinden commented to me that "There's no such thing as acting for the camera." Would you agree?*

ROEG: I'm not sure. I often change my mind about things like that. In casting I often find that everyone has something to offer. Absolutely everyone has a shine, a precociousness, or some interesting quality. You can make a decision after serious thought, or light thought. It may be a rather cavalier decision that can work. They can be pretty or they can be ugly—and you think, how charming!

O'BRIEN: *Can you comment on the actor and the role?*

ROEG: Actors can come to things too. I'd hate to twist someone's arm into doing a film. If an actor doesn't understand a script after reading it, if an actor doesn't get the *smell* of a role, you can't give it to him. With someone who has the smell, you know he has a backlog of experience. That will help develop a relationship with the role and with the director. Something in the actor can fulfill the part. In film there's a hidden quality in the performance that corresponds with the actor's backlog of experience.

O'BRIEN: *What about the first stages of the actor's preparations?*

ROEG: The actor must realize that no matter how much he thinks he knows about his role, he is only thinking of the external reality of the character. Once the actor is awakened, he can also see the dream inside the character. What the character really is. Then you have a connection.

WALTER MATTHAU

Actor: *Lonely Are the Brave, The Odd Couple, Charley Varrick*

O'BRIEN: *In your opinion, what is an actor psychologically?*

MATTHAU: An idiot posing as an artist.

O'BRIEN: *Do you believe in the idea that an actor has a "vocation" to act? Have you experienced the feeling of being called to act?*

MATTHAU: No. No.

O'BRIEN: *Vocation or not, what is the origin, or the deep motivations to which you attribute your choice of acting as a career?*

MATTHAU: Could not earn a living otherwise!

O'BRIEN: *Among the systems and theories of acting as an art, are there any you practice? Why?*

MATTHAU: The Matthau system. Because I know it best.

O'BRIEN: *Do you see any differences between the function and technique of the actor in film, and the actor in the other forms of drama?*

MATTHAU: No.

O'BRIEN: *What is the relationship between the actor and the film director? Is it constant or does it change or evolve from the temperament, the style, and the talent of the director?*

MATTHAU: The relationship *should* be that of equals. When it's not, the psychological forces of the individuals take over. That can be very good or very bad.

O'BRIEN: *If you were a film director, what would be your essential principles in directing an actor?*

MATTHAU: Leave him alone!

O'BRIEN: *What is the position of the actor in the working hierarchy of the film industry? What essential problems do you see? What solutions are there to these?*

MATTHAU: Depends on box office attraction. Endless. Impossible to discuss.

O'BRIEN: *What role does film criticism play in your life as an actor? Do you change your style according to the judgments of the critics?*

MATTHAU: None. No.

O'BRIEN: *Which of your film characterizations were the most challenging for you?*

MATTHAU: All of them.

O'BRIEN: *What is the most important advice you'd give a beginning film actor?*

MATTHAU: Don't do it.

AUSTIN PENDLETON

Actor and director: *What's Up Doc?*, *The Front Page*, *The Muppet Movie*, directed revival of *Little Foxes*

O'BRIEN: *How does the film actor maintain spontaneity and naturalness in take after take?*

PENDLETON: I think the way you keep what you're doing is by not trying to keep what you're doing. By thinking of each take as a new thing. Certain things, just by the logic of the scene, are going to come out the same, or at least have the same value or meaning. If you try to exactly repeat the moment or the behavior, it goes completely dry on you, I've found.

O'BRIEN: *So you try not to repeat?*

PENDLETON: You don't try not to repeat, you rewind and go back to the beginning. You try to stay alert to what's happening, alive to what's happening between you and who you're playing with.

O'BRIEN: *What do you think defines "quality" in an actor?*

PENDLETON: Authenticity. If a person is really using himself; that's not the same as playing himself, you know. But the actor is relating to the character that he or she is playing in a totally authentic way. They're not imposing either an idea of the character or, even worse, an idea of how they would like to be seen in the character. Within that you can do a wide range of characters. Because everyone has a wide range of things he can relate to. You're restricted somewhat by your own physicality or something like that, but you can relate in other ways emotionally and intellectually to a wide range of things. Along with this relating authentically to it without interfering or manipulating.

O'BRIEN: *What do you do about manipulating or interfering? Go along with it? Don't worry about it?*

PENDLETON: Go back to the partner. It's like you self-correct. You get extremely focused on the partner again and that brings you some new input to deal with and so then you're dealing again as opposed to manipulating.

O'BRIEN: *What do you mean by focus?*

PENDLETON: You just begin to take them in. Without asking them to have any particular effect on you. So, in other words, if you look at a partner and say, "Now I'm going to take you in right now because I want you to make me laugh or cry"—then that's manipulating them. But if you just say I'm going to take you in and you can have whatever effect on me you have, then it's all right.

O'BRIEN: *We don't really know much about how to get at the many layers, the variations within one human being—how to tap the resources. So is it the actor's work to do it on his own?*

PENDLETON: Actually I think there is a rehearsal technique, or in film, a technique of filming that can encompass that. In a rehearsal you can break apart a scene layer by layer, okay this time just play it for this, and do it a few times so it gets beyond just being an exercise, so that it really becomes internalized, and then after you've done that a few times, say okay let's play it this way a few times, let's bring out this level of conflict. Each time you try a new way, there's an overlay of the last way or ways that you've tried it. So by the time you're come to the tenth take or so, you have all these different layers going. Although you're only concentrating on one. I love that way of work. I found it is very releasing.

I think the way a lot of directors direct plays or film precludes the way of layering from being possible. So I do think it's the actor's work, but the actor has to be permitted to do it. You can't just do it at home in your head.

STACY KEACH

Actor: *Luther, Fat City, The Long Riders*

O'BRIEN: *In your opinion, what is an actor psychologically?*

KEACH: A lunatic who models men's behavior in a sane environment—a theatre, a set, before a camera or an audience.

O'BRIEN: *Do you believe in the idea that an actor has a "vocation" to act? Have you experienced the feeling of being called to act?*

KEACH: The calling came to me at about twelve or thirteen. I wanted to be so many people that only by choosing the career of "actor" could I be them all.

O'BRIEN: *Among the systems and theories of acting as an art, are there any you practice? Why?*

KEACH: Yes—for successful characterizations, *first visualize* what your goals are—looks, walk, sound of voice, then work towards your image.

O'BRIEN: *Do you see any differences between the function and technique of the actor in film, and the actor in the other forms of drama?*

KEACH: Film's prerequisite: *not* to act at all—to be "caught" behaving a certain way. *Eyes* important. Stage—*projection* of character via *voice*.

O'BRIEN: (A) *What is the relationship between the actor and the film director?*
(B) *Is it constant or does it change or evolve from the temperament, the style, and the talent of the director?*

KEACH: (A) Hopefully, good, but most often that of having to be "an ego-masseuse" or an extension of the director's vision—a "behaviorial model."
(B) It constantly changes.

O'BRIEN: *If you were a film director, what would be your essential principles in directing an actor?*

KEACH: To get them to do exactly what I want them to do, by trick or treat.

O'BRIEN: *What is the position of the actor in the working hierarchy of the film industry?*
What essential problems do you see?
What solutions are there to these?

KEACH: Usually, the producer (the money) has the final say (certainly in TV)—the director comes next—then the actor. The writer is low-man in TV, and film—the writer is higher in the theatre hierarchy.
None.
None.

O'BRIEN: *What role does film criticism play in your life as an actor?*
Do you change your style according to the judgments of the critics?

KEACH: Good reviews make you feel a lot better than bad
             ones—but best to take both with a grain of salt.
             Not if I can help it!

O'BRIEN: *Which of your film characterizations were the most challeng-
             ing for you?*

KEACH: South London Cop—*The Squeeze* (1976)
             English Industrialist—*Two Solitudes* (1977)
             Psychopathic Cop Killer—*Killer Inside Me* (1974)
             All *un*released films.

O'BRIEN: *What is the most important advice you'd give a beginning
             film actor?*

KEACH: Stay in shape—find other things to occupy your
             time—constantly develop new interests.

TOM COURTENAY

Actor: *The Loneliness of the Long Distance Runner, Billy Liar, King and
Country, Doctor Zhivago*

O'BRIEN: *Any advice for the young film actor?*

COURTENAY: Film is nerve-wracking because it's done in little bits
             and pieces. In theatre acting you have to save yourself
             for the evening's performance. But in film you have to
             stay ready the whole day. There are little bursts of
             intense activity, and then lots of waiting around in
             between. It's very hard on the nerves. I sometimes
             feel that people who do well on film are not so much
             accomplished actors, maybe, but have some look or
             presence or quality that the camera likes. Film actors
             have to develop a technique for spending the day. On
             a film it always takes a few days to adjust to the crew
             and the surroundings. And then of course you get into
             a rhythm, make friends with the crew. The atmos-
             phere should be as friendly as possible. I think that's
             important. So that people can be as relaxed as possi-
             ble, in these really quite nerve-wracking circumstanc-
             es. Especially in a small part. You never quite adjust

	. . . you're surrounded by people, and they're very close. You somehow forget they're doing a job, too. And you just feel they're watching you.
O'BRIEN:	*What film role has been your favorite? Is it the part you played in "King and Country?"*
COURTENAY:	Yes, but I realize that it didn't reach a wide public. I didn't expect to like the role so much as I did. I think I've more to offer now than I did before, because of my stage acting. I've developed as a comedian, developed timing playing in front of a live audience. So I would like to use that on the screen.
O'BRIEN:	*Would comedy be harder to do on the screen? It seems to me it would be harder to be comic than to be thoughtful.*
COURTENAY:	You can be both thoughtful and comic on screen. I think on the stage you have to have the thoughts clear, and then the emotions will come. It is interesting to see thinking. Either you've got that or you haven't. You can't feign it. It's either in you or it's not. But the actual thinking your way through it is important. If your mind is concentrated on the text, you'll impress it on the audience . . . much more.
O'BRIEN:	*How much intuition is involved?*
COURTENAY:	More than anything else. In the thing coming to life. You hope that will come, but I think it's good to think about the sense. If I have to read something, I always just plan to know where the full stops are, and what it means. I think that's the best thing. Then strange things happen when you come to do it. I've done concerts with singers, and I was so moved by the music. But I just spoke it as best I could. But I was only moved because I was moved; I didn't attempt to be moved. Working in film is moving out into the unknown. I mean the text of a play is solid. There it is. You can see it. And the part is much clearer. In a film you're much more at the mercy of the director.
O'BRIEN:	*Acting seems to be almost a religion, in that it's a worship of the wonder of life.*
COURTENAY:	Yes. It's also about magic. I've always thought that. But I believe you've got to do a bit of homework, and

then hopefully, the magic will happen. If you do all you can, you cast the thing, you approach the script with respect, and hopefully, vitality. Then something that is magical will happen.

MAGGIE SMITH

Actress: *The Prime of Miss Jean Brodie, Othello, California Suite*

O'BRIEN: *What is an actor, psychologically?*

SMITH: A figure in someone else's dream. The "someone else" could be the writer, the director, or the audience.

O'BRIEN: *Does the actor have a vocation to act? Have you experienced the feeling of being called to act?*

SMITH: Yes. I have never wanted to do anything else.

O'BRIEN: *Vocation or not, what is the origin, or the deep motivations to which you attribute your choice of acting as a career?*

SMITH: Imagination—originally inspired by reading; developed by growing up in Oxford.

O'BRIEN: *Among the systems and theories of acting as an art, are there any you practice? Why?*

SMITH: The Alexander Technique—as a means of preparation.

O'BRIEN: *Do you see any differences between the function and technique of the actor in film, and the actor in the other forms of drama?*

SMITH: The basis of any technique must be "Truth."

O'BRIEN: *What is the relationship between the actor and the film director?*

SMITH: All directors are different, therefore the relationships are always different.

O'BRIEN: *If you were a film director, what would be your essential techniques in directing an actor?*

SMITH: Create trust.

O'BRIEN: *What is the position of the actor in the working hierarchy of the film industry?*

SMITH: The actor is a pawn in the game. Movies are business.

	Nothing will ever change this—not in the U.S. or U.K., anyway.
O'BRIEN:	*What influence does film criticism have on your acting? Do you change your style according to the judgments of the critics?*
SMITH:	Film criticism has very little influence on my acting. It is always too late to change anything.
O'BRIEN:	*Which of your film characterizations offered the most challenge?*
SMITH:	Miss Brodie.
O'BRIEN:	*What is the most important advice you'd give a beginning film actor or actress?*
SMITH:	Make sure the cameraman is on your side. In the beginning it's how you look that counts. Later, the talent and skill will take care of the career.

SIR RALPH RICHARDSON

Actor: *The Fallen Idol, The Heiress, Richard III, Oh! What a Lovely War,*
Time Bandits

O'BRIEN:	*How would you describe film acting?*
RICHARDSON:	Although I'm more of a theatre actor than a film actor, I am very happy to act in films. It's like having your work put under the microscope. One tiny blink of an eye might do the work of waving the arm in the theatre.
	It's rather like doing a small lithograph or etching instead of a large painting or a bronze sculpture.

VERE LORRIMER

Director: BBC TV

O'BRIEN:	*What is an actor? Why does a person become an actor?*

LORRIMER: One who plays out our dreams at a remove. To continue the fantasies of childhood; to be loved for what one appears to be, rather than what one is!

O'BRIEN: *Certain directors declare they "love actors." Others see actors as puppets to be manipulated to serve the story. In which category are you?*

LORRIMER: I was an actor for 15 years—I love actors. They are our dreams made flesh, and need love and consideration. If you tend a flower you get beauty; if you manipulate a flower, you'll only get still life.

O'BRIEN: *What part does an actor play in the structure of a film, in comparison with the other collaborators on a film?*

LORRIMER: He plays an equal collaborative role with the writer, director, cameraman, and so on. But because cinema is a visual art, and the actor is the one we *see*, his role becomes paramount, ultimately the most important.

O'BRIEN: *How do you choose actors for your films? What qualities and techniques do you look for?*

LORRIMER: Strangely, for a visual medium, the most vital quality is *the voice*. Think of Bogart, Garbo, Gable, Hurt, Tracy, etc. It is the *voice* that makes an actor truly memorable.

O'BRIEN: *During the course of making a film, what kind of relationship do you establish with an actor?*

LORRIMER: *Mutual trust*—but only one man can be boss: the director. But actors come up with many a good idea. The smart director will recognize and assimilate such ideas. The director is the molder—and guardian—of an actor's performance.

O'BRIEN: *Do you follow the principles established by any film theorist or film director in directing actors? What are your essential principles in directing actors?*

LORRIMER: All actors are *individuals*. Some need direction. Some need guidance. Some need encouragement. Some need pushing. Some are so good they don't need any direction. To ignore the experience of the great and gifted directors is foolish. So read Eisenstein and Paul Rotha, and never stop learning.

O'BRIEN: *What directors and films do you consider exemplary for the direction of actors?*

LORRIMER: Hitchcock: storytelling; Cukor: women; Siegal: crime; Lucas: invention; Lean: epic; Capra: humour; Welles: panache; Chaplin: comedy; Corman: energy; Hathaway: workmanship; Altman: changing taste; Mervyn Le Roy: know-how; Ford: Americana; and Howard Hawks: everything!

O'BRIEN: *In film history, which actors do you consider were the best for acting before the camera?*

LORRIMER: MEN: Chaplin, Bogart, Cagney, Gable, Rathbone, Laughton, Rooney, Robinson, Olivier, Jouvet, Gabin, Mastroianni, Astaire, and Guinness.
WOMEN: Garbo, Gish, Davies, Hayward, Hepburn, Rogers, Dame Edith Evans, Giulietta Masina, and Monroe.

O'BRIEN: *When you are a spectator, what do you look for in a film actor?*

LORRIMER: A riveting personality.

MICHAEL MURPHY

Actor: *The Front, Manhattan, The Autobiography of Miss Jane Pittman*

O'BRIEN: *Why does a person act?*

MURPHY: A lot of different reasons. A lot of them do it for a need to be recognized—celebrity—a need to get outside themselves.

O'BRIEN: *In ancient Greece the theatre artists were called "poets". Actors create a poetry of human behavior.*

MURPHY: That's the aspect that interests me most—behavior— to see how people behave and interpret that. Whether you like me or not in a movie doesn't concern me too much.

O'BRIEN: *Can you collaborate with the director and the writer on most film work?*

MURPHY: I've been able to, mostly because I've worked with good people. The outstanding part of my career is the people I've worked with. The better the director generally, the more of a collaboration it is. The more insecure a guy is, the more of a martinet he is.

O'BRIEN: *Do you ever make suggestions as to camera angle or tracking?*

MURPHY: Yeah. I never insist on anything, but make suggestions all the time. I might say, "That's a hard way to do this." They have to take what you're doing into consideration. Again, most of these guys are fairly flexible. Occasionally you run into somebody who's got every shot planned before the picture is started. I don't see the actor in any kind of subservient role, any more than I see the director or producer in a subservient role.

O'BRIEN: *After you read the script, do you start thinking about makeup, wardrobe, or costume?*

MURPHY: Yes, it's very important, I think. I try to find a little something that puts it over the top of my head, what I should like.

O'BRIEN: *What kind of something?*

MURPHY: Anything. Jewelry. Something that is typical for this person, that rings a bell in my head. It's not always the look either, but that's a big help. Sometimes it's just a clue.

O'BRIEN: *Some acting depends on a lot of little clues?*

MURPHY: Yes. You just think about it and think about it. You're walking to the post office one morning and suddenly something dawns on you.

O'BRIEN: *Some screen performances are manipulative in their naturalness.*

MURPHY: True. It's dangerous because you've got to go a long way to get there. If you don't do that character work, it's not enough to just look natural, or relaxed. It's soap opera acting, fake natural. I'm not putting down soap actors, but most scenes are unplayable with god-awful dialogue. Everybody's saying forty-seven proper names in one sentence. You have four different things going against you. They're shot badly. The lighting is so terrible that you're always reminded that these people are actors. There's no atmosphere on the screen. There you sit, with 4,000 lights on you. You're sweating and saying this impossible dialogue trying to be cool, and it's hard.

O'BRIEN: *They're very low-key on soap operas.*

MURPHY: But it's that kind of manipulative behaviorist acting you're talking about. First of all, you have to be sure that what you have to say is playable. You want to be in a picture that has some kind of atmosphere to it. Most of the time you're going to go through life and there'll be three or four things that are acceptable and the rest are—well, you do the best you can.

KING VIDOR

Director: *The Crowd, The Big Parade, Our Daily Bread, The Fountainhead*

O'BRIEN: *What is an actor? Why does a person become an actor?*

VIDOR: Although I have had many dealings with all kinds of actors, I don't know whether I have established a notion that would answer the two questions. Tentatively, it appears to me that it is connected with some sort of what one might say neuroticism that begs to be expressed and seeks a response or reward in some sort of appreciation or applause. Of course in the present day it is a well-paid job, and this element no doubt plays a large part. But I think the successful actor is motivated by the desire to express his individuality or personality and decides on this medium as the best to accomplish his desires.

O'BRIEN: *Certain directors declare they "love actors." Others see actors as puppets to be manipulated to serve the story. In which category are you?*

VIDOR: I never have seen actors as puppets. I have always visualized my relationship with actors as a two-way street, meaning that they should give to the project at hand as much as we give them. In other words, we give them the part and the work we have done on the part, the story, and the direction, etc., and they give us not just a body but an individuality, a personality. If they bring to the part or to the film no more than just a body, a physical object, I have no use for them. They have to contribute and represent all that they stand for as individuals.

O'BRIEN: *Within the structure of a film, what part does an actor play, in comparison with the other collaborators on a film?*

VIDOR: I believe it is possible to perhaps extract a performance from someone who knows nothing about acting, but the closeness of the camera and the enlargement of the image relatively shows up this deficiency. Actually, I believe that each individual has something to say, but the ability to express this and the medium through which it is expressed is the best definition of an artist that I know of. In other words, what good is the makeup of an individual if he can't convey something of his viewpoint to a film camera or an audience? It takes courage, it takes technique to be able to find the proper medium and express it. My viewpoint of a film is that it is a structure of many parts. It is the director who brings all these parts together under his interpretation and makes them into one definite whole.

I remember when I was starting out very young making films, I directed a picture with Laurette Taylor, *Peg O' My Heart*. She had played the part many years in the theatre, but when I worked on the script without ever having seen her in the play or without ever having seen the play, I had many preconceptions of what the part should be. But when I met her and saw what sort of person she was and what sort of comedienne or actress she was, I realized I had to adapt my thoughts to her mannerisms, character, and so forth. I changed my rigid concepts to suit the valid qualities of the star. In other cases I have found instances where I have made the actor conform to the concepts of the screenplay of the particular character he is playing. I think in both cases the validity and integrity of the actor himself cannot be underestimated. It is a large part of the entire structure.

O'BRIEN: *What is the relationship between the actor and the film director? Is it constant or does it change or evolve from the temperament, the style, and the talent of the director?*

VIDOR: Now that you bring up the question, it makes for an interesting reply. An actor is playing a part, not necessarily himself. He is there because the director is looking at him as that character. It seems to me that a very close relationship between director and actor, particularly of a star quality, tends to somewhat destroy this relationship. I have known many instances where a star, while playing a certain part, has kept in the mood of that part throughout all of his waking hours at home or in the studio. This is to be encouraged.

O'BRIEN: *What are your essential principles in directing an actor?*

VIDOR: I have said to my friend Andrew Wyeth about filmmaking, I wanted everything to look real but not necessarily to be real. The whole activity of filmmaking is done by an illusion of movement which is not actually there, so that filmmaking is based on an illusion. The process is an artistic one. This goes for acting as well as directing, and for the relationship between the two. I do not follow any principles established by any film theorists or great film director. I have been associated with films almost from the beginning, and I have had to establish my own methods and techniques.

CHRISTOPHER BARRY

Director: BBC TV series *Poldark*

O'BRIEN: *What is the process after you have received a script to direct, and you meet the actors for the first time?*

BARRY: The normal technique for a studio production is that
we will meet at a rehearsal hall, which we have here at
the BBC, and all come and sit around the table, and
have a read-through. Of course, first of all, we
introduce everyone, and then we read the script
through with a stop watch and get some idea of the
running time. Then we start in to block the scenes,
and the rehearsal hall is pegged out with colored tapes
on the floor for sizes of the actual sets that they're
going to be working in, working areas with rough
furniture and rough props.

I work with a blueprint, a skeleton of my camera
script already prepared, because I prefer then to work
from that, and vary it, change things as we go along.
Just the fact that it has concentrated my mind as to the
way we're going. During that process if an actor wants
to vary a move significantly, so that it changes what
I've got marked down, then I amend it. In fact, I find
that I'm rubbing out things in my script, because I
constantly do need to make additions if things don't
work out the way I planned them exactly. Obviously,
one sees, as one comes into rehearsal, one sees looks,
one gets nuances that one hadn't realized before were
going to happen.

O'BRIEN: *What kind of collaboration do you have with actors?*
BARRY: On the whole, I think I have very good working
relationships with actors. Actors tend to respect and
like me. I'm not an ego-trip man, trying to do it my
way. And I have a lot of collaboration with them.

Obviously, in television, the sort of work I do,
which is not the sort of single play with long rehearsals, because of the technicalities, there is a certain
dictatorship needed by the fact that you've only got
eight days to rehearse and put on an hour's show. And
in that time, you've not just got to rehearse the actors
in their parts; you've got to have a shooting script
ready to go into the studio, and knock it off in two
days in the studio. One has got to be to an extent
dictatorial, and have the final say; that doesn't mean to

say one has to wear jackboots and carry a whip. There are better ways of doing things. I've always found if you give actors a reason for doing something they'll listen. If you tell actors, you want to record two scenes out of order because if you do that, it saves a costume change, even though it puts their big scene, their difficult scene, before their easier scene, they're usually amenable. They'll say, "Well, if you've got to do it that way; I, too, am prepared to listen."

O'BRIEN: *If an actor suggested a camera angle or a camera movement to you, would you be open to that?*

BARRY: Very rarely has an actor done that. They'll suggest actors' moves, which may be very relative to camera; it may have the same effect as a camera angle, ultimately, in fact, if it's bringing him into close-up, or something. If he's got reasons for suggesting it, and it overrides my reasons for asking him to do something different, then I'm perfectly prepared to discuss it with him. But if it balls up the whole scene, dramatically or just technically, making it impossible for me to shoot it, then I would try to dissuade him from that persistence, and try to convince him that my way is right. Very often I find, particularly with actors who wish to assert themselves, and these are probably not your best actors, but middle-range actors, when you give them something, they say, "No, no, I want to do it this way." I say, "Well, go on, try it." And they'll try it, and generally speaking, they'll come back and say, "No, I think your way works better." And that's just because one (the director) has thought it out, and with such a short time period, one doesn't want to mess about. It may not be the best way, but ultimately it's a way for everyone to settle down and get on with it.

O'BRIEN: *Do you think an outdoor location is more stimulating for the actor? Is there any advantage to the actor in being forced to deal with a real environment?*

BARRY: If you mean by that, sitting in a cheesecloth shirt on a freezing cliff playing a love scene, it's quite a strain. In

Poldark, Robin Ellis and Angharad Rees . . . I remember in one scene we were filming . . . *we* were all wrapped up in our long johns and big anoraks, and they were literally in a howling gale on the cliff's edge. All he had next to his skin was a thin cotton shirt. We had to build a windbreak just to keep it off them. It's a hell of a test for actors. I'm always remarkably impressed with the way they manage to bring it off. I don't think it's particularly kind to them, I don't think it necessarily produces the best performance.

I think there's a great tendency in drama, now particularly, and it's going to come in more and more, is what we call electronic production in the field. This means taking small cameras out on location, rather than using film for inserts, or filming the whole thing. Smaller cameras, which carry their own packs. These can be taken out very easily on location, shooting with two cameras at once. And of course, the inevitable compromise comes with electronic shooting, when you've got two cameras going simultaneously, compromising angles, but possibly better for performance. The actors can keep going through long chunks of dialogue. This electronic shooting is growing more and more, and I think the actors like that.

CAROL SCOTT

Location Casting Director: *Sharky's Machine, Roots, Palmerstown, U.S.A.*

O'BRIEN: *What is the process of location casting?*
SCOTT: In the normal sequence of events, I receive a script in the mail. Usually there is a breakdown of the characters in the script. Sometimes I have to do the breakdown; occasionally the producer will have it done by a service.

           After we've negotiated the deal, I usually get the

script a couple of weeks before the director arrives. The script breakdown tells what characters are needed. I read the script to get a feel for it, and usually talk to the director about the parts that must be cast locally. Some minor roles may be cast locally. We discuss what he has in mind for each character. Sometimes there's a lot of leeway in casting: the director might be willing to consider several different types for the roles. Sometimes he doesn't have a preconceived notion, and sometimes he will change his mind during the process of discussion or casting.

After several conversations with the director, I'm ready to start looking for people. There are certain guidelines set out by the Screen Actor's Guild (SAG) which must be followed during the process. First of all, I must interview every SAG actor who could qualify for each of the roles. And I must exhaust the SAG possibilities before I can cast a nonunion actor.

I contact the union agents in town and have meetings with them about the parts that are available. If the agents have talent that is appropriate, we will set up a series of interviews.

O'BRIEN: *What happens during an interview with the actor?*

SCOTT: I select a key scene from the script for each character I'm casting. Then I give out copies of these in advance to the actors so that they'll have time to prepare for the reading. If there are actors that I'm familiar with, I usually don't have them go through this first interview process. It can be an agonizing experience. Usually, the first interview is for SAG actors I haven't met yet. Records have to be kept on these interviews. The amount of time, for instance, is important because union actors cannot be kept waiting more than an hour. Often the production company can be fined if actors are kept waiting beyond an hour's time. I enjoy meeting these actors because it can be very exciting discovering someone for the first time for a role.

Then I audition all the actors before the director arrives and try to narrow down the field. I like to present the director with three or four actors for each role. Sometimes an actor is suitable for two or three of the roles we're trying to fill.

After we read some people with the director, he sometimes changes his mind about the direction we're going in, and decides to try something else.

O'BRIEN: *What do you look for when you're interviewing an actor?*

SCOTT: I first look at the headsheet with the information about their training and experience. I'm partial to actors with a good, solid theatrical background training in theatre.

I refuse to see any actor who comes in without the headsheet: the photo and resume. If I'm seeing 30 or 40 people a day, there's no way I can remember someone without a photograph that I can keep. It's very unprofessional to come to an interview without a photograph and resume. At the very least, actors should bring in a simple polaroid. Unless I have a photograph, there's no way to recall the actor. This should be stressed.

Usually I talk to the actors first, try to find out something about their backgrounds until they're at ease, and not so nervous about the reading. I like to know who they are. That helps me remember them, too. They may tell me some story about themselves that will stick with me.

I hate cold readings, so I try to give the actors enough time to look over the material. The reading takes only a short time; it's usually just a couple of pages from the script. If I like what I've seen, I ask the actor to do it a second time and ask for a different interpretation, even though he may have been right on the money the first time. What I'm trying to find out is how directable the actors are. Can they do the reading more than one way? Are they simply one-dimensional or can they take direction and change the interpretation easily? If they can only do it one way, that's not too good.

After the interviews and readings, I usually get

back with the director and tell him what I've found. I like to keep the director informed on the progress; he doesn't usually like surprises. I'll let him know if I have the right actors, or if I'm having difficulty with any role.

The next step after the prescreening and narrowing of the field is to set up interviews with the director. The actor comes in; I introduce him to the director, and depending upon how much time we have, the director may use the same technique of putting the actor at ease before starting the reading.

Several techniques can be used during these readings. I've had a lot of luck letting the actor come in and do a short piece from some show he's already done. Being familiar with the scene, the actor can look really good. It usually impresses the director; this sort of thing is not usually done in Hollywood casting. It depends on the amount of time we have. I tell the actor to choose a piece that is in character with the type of role that we're trying to cast. This kind of reading often shows the actor's range better than a reading of a couple of lines in the script we're casting.

After we've seen everyone, we lay the photographs out and discuss the actors, the possibilities of each one, and try to narrow it down to a couple of people. Sometimes the director knows immediately which actors he wants to cast. Sometimes we just haven't found the right actor for the particular role, and have to keep looking. Each film is different and each director makes different demands. Some directors exercise great care in casting even the smallest roles. For example, we often prepare for casting by spending time researching documentaries or newsfilms of the period.

After the actual casting is accomplished, I provide information for the actors' contracts. I also clear the actor's standing with SAG. If an actor is not a member of SAG, I prepare a Taft-Hartley form explaining why I chose this actor. In addition to paying the actor the current scale rate for a day player, the producer has to pay a percentage of the rate to the actor's agent. This percentage is not deducted from the actor's fee, which is an advantage for the actor. During the contract negotiations, we also make deals for the billing or screen credit.

O'BRIEN: *Does the director always audition every actor you cast?*

SCOTT: We're using videotape more and more in casting. I can send a director a videotape of an actor that we might be interested in, and cast him from the tape. If I see an actor at work in another city, for instance, I can forward a tape to the director who might be on location and unavailable for an interview. That bit of technology is becoming more and more important in the film industry.

INDEX